When Harry Met Sandra

When
Harry
Met
Sandra

More than 50 years of
marriage, love, life and strife

HARRY AND SANDRA REDKNAPP

MIRROR BOOKS

m
B

MIRROR BOOKS

1

First published in Great Britain and Ireland in 2022 by
Mirror Books, a Reach PLC business,
5 St Paul's Square, Liverpool, L3 9SJ.

www.mirrorbooks.co.uk
@TheMirrorBooks

Hardback ISBN: 9781915306029
eBook ISBN: 9781915306036

Photographic acknowledgements:
The Redknapp family, Alamy, Reach Plc.

Every effort has been made to trace copyright.
Any oversights will be rectified in future editions.

Design and production by Mirror Books.
Design and typesetting by Danny Lyle.

Printed and bound by CPI Group (UK) Ltd,
Croydon, CR0 4YY.

Contents

Prologue

Together forever

*'I'm not going to let you go,
you're not going anywhere.
You can come in my hammock!'*

Harry

I'm pretty old school. I am not ashamed to say that I am much more comfortable in the company of men, and I am not one of these people who greet people with a kiss or a cuddle. And I don't cry. Well, I hadn't cried until 2018 – and that just happened to be in front of millions of people.

I had been in the *I'm a Celebrity* jungle for almost three weeks when I was called up to the Bush Telegraph. I can only describe the telegraph as a dark, small shed. Inside, it had a bench, a large black wall with a camera and a producer behind it, and a few insects who had made their way through the gaps.

"You've gotta leave the camp, you've gotta go," they said.

"Where am I going?" I asked the black wall in front of me.

"You need to go immediately," came the reply.

Suddenly I feared the worst. Sandra had the life-threatening infection sepsis just weeks before I flew out to Australia, and I only went into the jungle on the condition she was well enough. But now I was terrified she wasn't. 'What have I done?' I thought to myself. 'Sandra is obviously not well at all.'

I had a terrible feeling that something really bad had happened. It felt like my heart had hit my stomach.

"Why have I got to go immediately?" I asked. I could hear the panic in my own voice. I was hoping the voice behind the screen was going to give me some reassurance.

But, "Please, you need to leave" was the reply that came back. "You need to go down the path, don't turn right back into the camp, instead take a left, cross the bridge and then go down the stairs."

"Can I go and get my stuff?" I asked.

"No," they said bluntly.

"What about my water bottle?" I replied.

"No, you just need to leave now. A producer is waiting for you."

Now I am really worried. Why does a producer want to meet me and why outside of camp? This hasn't happened to anyone else? What the hell is going on?

I got up and quickly walked down the path, probably a slow jog, I took the left and ran across the bridge, and, as you can imagine, I had all sorts of things going through my mind. My head is a busy place at the best of times, but if it is anything that concerns Sandra, I just go into a panic.

I quickly made my way down the stairs, trying to find the producer. There is no one here. I walked through a bush and there she was.

"Sarn!!" I cried. Literally!

Just seeing her sitting on that rock and she was okay, well, it just did me in. My eyes filled up with tears.

"You didn't know that I was coming, did you?" Sandra said, with a big smile across her face.

"I'm not going to let you go, you're not going anywhere. You can come in my hammock!" I told her as I squeezed her tight. Then the tears started falling.

"I can't help this, it is not like me, I don't normally cry, I am pretty old school. Are you pleased to see me?" I asked her.

I think it was a shock for Sandra to see me like that, really. She will say I don't ever show my emotions easily – well, certainly not tears anyway.

Before I went into the jungle I had to go and see a woman in London to check I was mentally prepared for camp life and I got asked all sorts of questions.

"Have you got a bad temper?" was one.

"No, not really," I replied.

"What makes you lose your temper then?" she asked.

"Losing a game, but then I get over it," I replied.

"If someone upset you in camp, would you hit them?" came the next question.

"Hit them? Absolutely not!" I told her.

"Would you hit a woman?" she asked.

"No!" This was becoming silly now, I thought. "Why would I hit a woman? Never in a million years," came my response.

She looked back at her notebook, then looked up. "How do you handle emotion?"

"What do you mean?" I asked.

"Well, for instance, do you ever cry?"

"Cry? No, you must be joking, not me. I don't do crying!" I told her.

I definitely underestimated what being away from Sandra would do to me. I would have given you odds of a million to one for me to cry in the jungle. But Sandra and I have hardly been apart in five decades of marriage, so not being able to make contact with her was very difficult for me. I am totally besotted with her and I love spending time with her – being away from Sandra feels strange to me. I am lost.

"I got a bit sad the other day," she said to me during her surprise visit to the jungle. "I got a bit tearful because I missed you."

'Sarn, what are you doing to me?' I thought. I hated knowing she was upset.

We carried on talking for a bit more on the log before the producer came along.

"It is time to go back in now, Harry," he said.

As you can imagine it was difficult for me to say goodbye to Sandra, probably more so than when I left Bournemouth to fly to Australia, but I felt very lucky that I got to be with her for half an hour that day. Seeing her in the flesh and knowing she was okay after all that time apart really did lift me.

I walked back into the Bush Telegraph and sat myself back on the familiar wooden bench in front of the familiar black screen, a familiar insect making its way up my leg.

"It is funny, 54 years and we just don't want to be apart," I told the blank wall. "That has done me up today, I have missed her so much. I love you so much!"

This year marked our 55th wedding anniversary, and 58 years since we first met. In some ways it feels like yesterday since I first set eyes on Sandra in the Two Puddings pub in Stratford, but in other ways, we have been together for a lifetime.

Once you hit it off with someone, you just know, don't you? And I knew from the very moment that I met Sandra that I wanted to be with her for the rest of my life, though if I am honest, I am not sure she would say the same thing about me! We just get on so, so well together and we love being in each other's company and spending time together.

People have often asked us over the years what the secret to our marriage is and I can't answer that question. I don't think there is a secret. I can't say there is one thing – I just fell in love with her and she fell in love with me. We are very lucky; I am very lucky.

Chapter 1

Can I have your number?

'He might have been good on his feet on the football pitch, but definitely not on the dance floor'

Sandra

It is hard to believe it was almost 60 years ago, and I know it is a cliché, but I still remember the night I first met Harry as if it was yesterday. It was the summer of 1964 and it had been a warm and bright Sunday. Dressed in a pink sleeveless shift dress and kitten heels, my friend Susan and I made our way from my parents' house in Barking to the Two Puddings, a pub in Stratford, east London.

"I'm looking forward to having a dance tonight," I told Susan as I applied another coat of pink lipstick.

I was only 17, but we were regulars at the disco above the pub. We loved it there as they would play Motown records all night and we would dance around our handbags. I would always be wearing a shift dress, that was my go-to outfit, and my drink was port and lemon, which I would have in a wine glass as that was quite fashionable back then.

I remember Susan and I were chatting away near the bar when two smartly dressed men approached us.

"Would you like to dance?" one said to me.

I never used to be attracted to anyone who was shorter than me. When I was at school I was the tallest girl in my class, so I was always quite conscious of my height. But the man standing in front of me in a pressed grey suit and tie looked a fairly good height. 'At least he is taller than me,' I thought to myself.

"My name is Harry," he said with a smile as his friend, Colin, took Susan by the hand and started twirling her around the dance floor. "Okay then," I said, feeling quite shy.

Harry wasn't much of a dancer. He might have been good on his feet on the football pitch, but definitely not on the dance floor. I remember he trod on my toes more than a few times! But then I wasn't that great of a mover either. I was also very shy and wasn't ever one for attention, especially from men.

As the night drew to a close, people started to gather their coats.

"Can I give you a lift home?" Harry asked.

"That would be nice, thank you," I replied.

We left the Two Puddings and walked out to Harry's car. It was a little green one, a Morris 1100, I think it was.

"Where do you live?" he asked, opening the passenger door for me.

"Barking," I told him. He nodded. "Nice area," he replied.

I don't remember too much from the journey home other than Harry talking about football.

"I play for the West Ham youth team," he said, two hands on the wheel. "We are playing in the FA Youth Cup. It will be on TV, if you want to watch it."

If he thought I was going to be impressed, I wasn't. I wasn't interested in football at all.

Pulling up outside my parents' house, I reached down to the footwell to pick up my handbag. I was about to thank Harry for the lift when he turned to face me.

"Umm, I don't suppose I could ask for your number, could I?"

"Yes, go on then," I said, opening my handbag and reaching for my pink lipstick. I grabbed a piece of cardboard and wrote down my number. 01 594 1254. It is funny how old family phone numbers stay with you after all these years, isn't it?

"Thanks," he said, taking the cardboard from my hand and putting it in the pocket of his suit jacket. "I'll give you a call."

"Thanks Harry," I said, opening the door. "It has been nice to meet you."

I can say this now as Harry and I have often joked about it over the years, but when I handed him my number I wasn't that fussed if he called me or not – it wasn't like it was love at first sight. And to be honest, I really didn't expect to ever see or hear from Harry again as I didn't think he was that interested in me either.

A few days later, I bumped into a friend. Her dad was a coach down at West Ham.

"I heard you were out with one of the players the other night," she said with a smile. "The ginger one."

"Harry? He is not ginger!" I laughed.

"Yeah, Harry Redknapp, he has got ginger hair," she said. "Anyway, how did it go? Are you seeing him again?"

As a hairdresser I would come across all shades of hair, so I remember feeling embarrassed that I couldn't even remember his hair colour!

"Erm, I doubt it," I told her. "But he has got my number."

It took a good couple of weeks for Harry to call me. If you asked Harry how long it took him, he would say it was only a week, but it was definitely longer.

Back then we had a party line at home which we shared with our neighbours across the road. I remember there being times when I would pick up the phone to make a call to a friend and hear someone from the other family chatting away, so I would quickly have to hang up and wait for them to get off.

Can I have your number?

That is how it was in the Sixties. I lived in a terraced house with my mum, Betty, my dad, Bill, my older brother Brian and younger sister Patricia. We were all at home when the phone rang.

"Hi Sandra, how are you doing?" It was Harry. "Would you like to come to a party with me? One of my team-mates is having a do to celebrate his birthday and I would really like it if you could come."

"Er, I am not sure. Who will be there?" I asked.

"Me, a few West Ham players, their girlfriends, I will introduce you. It should be fun," he said.

The thought of spending the night with a bunch of footballers didn't really excite me, if I am honest – some of my friends would have loved it, they were all West Ham fans! But I had no interest in the game, and despite living a stone's throw away from Upton Park, my dad and brother weren't interested in football either. But Harry seemed nice, and if he was nice, his friends are bound to be, so I agreed.

"Okay," I told Harry. "I'll come with you."

That night, Harry came to pick me up in his little green car and we made our way to the party. "This is Sandra," he said, introducing me to his friends.

We all chatted throughout the night and I noticed Harry was becoming more and more drunk. He told me he wasn't a beer drinker and so he had been on the Bacardi and cokes.

5

"I don't feel that well," he slurred.

'Why has he got himself in such a state?' I remember thinking to myself. Maybe it was the nerves, I really didn't know, but he was so drunk, there was no way he was going to be able to drive.

Harry's friend, Johnny George, turned to me. "Don't worry Sandra, I will drop you home," he said. "Harry doesn't usually get like this. I am not sure what is the matter with him."

There was one thing I knew, and that was that I didn't want to see Harry again, not if he was going to get himself in such a state on a night out.

It wasn't until a few days later when my sister Pat told me she was dating one of Harry's team-mates, a chap called Frank Lampard, and said that she had heard Harry was a good man that I had a change of heart.

'Maybe I will see him again,' I thought to myself.

Chapter 2

Meet the parents

'Sandra had finally forgiven me for a disastrous night at my mate's birthday party when I got rotten drunk. What a nightmare'

Harry

Growing up in a council flat on the Burdett Estate in Poplar, East London, we didn't have much money. I was an only child and lived with my mum, Violet, and dad, Harry Sr. I might have been playing for the youth team at West Ham when I was 17, but it was different back then. You certainly weren't getting wages like the kids get these days.

I have loved football for as long as I can remember. I got the love from my dad, for sure, in fact, he probably loved it more than me. My dad was absolutely football-mad. I was just six

7

years old when he took me to watch my first game at Millwall. I was so little, I remember standing on a small box just so I could be a bit taller and watch the game. He was a big Arsenal fan and he would catch two buses to every game; he was that committed. He would get the 106, then change to the 277, and he did that every Saturday for as long as I can remember. Sometimes he would take me along, and although we didn't have a lot of money, he always made sure we had enough to get a cheese roll and a cup of tea.

His favourite player was a bloke called Jimmy Logie. He was a Scottish fella who played up front for Arsenal. He used to sell newspapers close to where we lived, because back then footballers didn't just play football, they had proper jobs too. My dad would go and find Jimmy to buy a newspaper from him, just so he could see him and have a chat.

But Arsenal wasn't his greatest love; what my dad loved the most was watching us all have a kickabout around the estate. He would go out on the balcony and just watch us. When I was at West Ham, he would come and watch us train every week and come to every game. I remember introducing my dad to one of my mates at West Ham.

"Oh I know you," he said, looking up to my old man. "You used to watch us from the touchline every Sunday."

Football was so different to what it is now. There were no replica kits for the fans to wear; they became popular much later, especially from the Eighties. You wouldn't get a football shirt for Christmas, there was no such thing. If you went to watch Tottenham Hotspur play in the Sixties, the only people in Tottenham kits were the players. All the fans in the crowd would be smartly dressed, and wearing shirts or suits with flat caps. The players would go for a drink in the local pub after a game; there was no glamour to the game at all.

My dad was over the moon when I signed for West Ham as a winger in 1962 and one of my first big matches was playing in the FA Youth Cup. Like my dad, I would get the bus everywhere and would get the bus to training every day. It took me an hour and a half to get down to our training ground in Chadwell Heath and I did that every day until I could afford to buy my first car, a green Morris 1100.

One day I was driving along with my mate, Eddie Bovington, when he said, "I have heard you've been taking a blonde bird out from that hair salon in Barking, the good-looking one."

Sandra and I had been courting for a couple of months by this point. I had met her in the Two Puddings earlier that summer.

"I fancy the blonde one," I told my mate Colin, before walking over and asking her for a dance.

Sandra had also finally forgiven me for a disastrous night at my mate's birthday party when I got absolutely rotten drunk. What a nightmare that was!

"I am sorry," I sheepishly told her over the phone a few days later. "Can I take you out again?"

"I can't believe your mate had to take me home, Harry," she said, before taking in a breath. "But okay, yes, I don't mind going out with you again." The conversation didn't leave me totally convinced that she liked me, but at least she agreed.

By this time, my best mate at West Ham, Frank Lampard, was dating Sandra's younger sister Pat, and if I am honest, I think that went a long way in helping my cause. Frank was a bit younger than me, also a footballer, and a very good-looking fella. It didn't surprise me that he had a girlfriend, all the girls loved him.

I remember one day he came up to me in the dressing room at Chadwell Heath.

"I met a girl at the Ship in Stepney last night and you are seeing her sister," he said.

"Never," I told him. I couldn't believe it. What were the chances?

"Her name is Patricia, she is Sandra's little sister," he said.

If I am honest, if it wasn't for the two of them getting together, I am not sure Sandra would have ever given me another chance. But thank God she did!

Pat was lovely, a diamond of a lady. All of Sandra's family were lovely. I remember meeting her mum and dad for the first time. Her dad, Bill Harris, was a foreman down at Albert

Meet the parents

Dock. He was a big old fella, huge in fact. Built like a rugby player with broad shoulders and big arms and legs. And her brother Brian wasn't far behind him. You wouldn't want to mess with Bill Harris, that is for sure, but he was a lovely man.

I remember when I would drive to pick Sandra up for a night out or to drop her back home, I would always pop into the house to say hello to her parents, have a cup of tea and watch TV. It was usually Coronation Street. I wasn't a fan then and I am certainly not now, but Sandra has always been into it.

After about 10 minutes or so, Bill would start banging on the floor from the bedroom directly above us.

"It is time to go," he would shout, and that was it, off I went. I guess he thought we might be getting up to something, but no chance, not in those days you didn't! It was like another world.

Sandra's mum and dad's house was very, very different to mine. I thought they were quite posh to have their own house. We lived on the fourth floor of a tower block on a council estate. Our neighbours were the people who lived in the 17 other blocks.

Before we moved to the Burdett Estate we lived at my great-grandmother's house – Granny Cooper I called her – on Barchester Street. She didn't have a bathroom, but an outside toilet and a tin bath that would be hung up on the wall in the yard. Once a week you'd bring it in and that was bath night. She let my mum have two bedrooms at the top of her house and we stayed there until we moved to the Burdett.

My mum's dad worked in the docks all his life and my nan looked after the home. I remember my mum would get up to go to work early and my nan would get me out of bed and off to school and have my dinner waiting for me on the table when I got home. She was an absolutely fantastic lady, my old nan. She was also a terrible gambler and loved horse racing – I am sure I inherited it from her. She helped out the local bookmaker, Cyril, by getting horse bets off all the old girls in the streets. Two bob here, two bob there. Then Cyril would turn up once a week – always in a trilby hat, a pressed shirt, tie, suit and shiny shoes, and he would collect the bets from my nan. She had a fair few bets herself, too.

"Pick a horse," she would tell me, giving me a pencil. I couldn't read, so I would just dig the pencil in the paper. She would then rub the piece of paper on the top of my head. "Ginger for luck," she would say.

If anyone won, which did include my nan a few times, Cyril would be back and my nan would be dishing out their two bobsworth.

It all seemed quite fun and innocent, but betting was totally illegal. There were no betting shops. I was having my dinner one night and my nan got loaded into the back of a police car!

"Don't worry boy, finish your dinner, I won't be long," she would say when it happened. And she never was. They would take her down to the station, give her a slap on the wrist and let her go. Then the next week she would be back down Poplar Station having a telling off by the local bobby. And then the following week Cyril would be nicked.

We didn't have a lot, but no one did. I remember my mum and dad had a nine-inch television with a three-inch magnifying glass over it to make it a 12-inch! You had barely any channels and the only football match you'd see on TV was the FA Cup final. We would even listen to the Grand National all sat around the radio. I loved doing that with my nan.

Looking back, I think Sandra was probably a bit nervous about introducing me to her mum and dad and was worried whether they would like me or not. Her house always seemed busier than mine. I was an only child, but she was one of three. I remember her dear old dad would cook us all a big Sunday roast − usually a joint of beef with lovely roast potatoes. Bill was a brilliant cook. I am sure Sandra would tell you it is a shame it didn't rub off on me!

But Sandra's family were very welcoming and such lovely people, every single one of them. They didn't care where I lived or where I came from. And the most important thing was, neither did Sandra.

Chapter 3

Wrapped in cotton wool

*'Oh good, he is nice and clean,' I
remember telling my mum.
'He washes his hands after using the toilet.'*

Sandra

I never really had boyfriends, that wasn't the sort of thing you did back then. I was more interested in going out with my friends after work and having a dance on a weekend.

I am quite a shy person. I don't like attention and would prefer to go under the radar. My mum was very protective of us growing up. I guess you could say she wrapped us all up in cotton wool. My dad, Bill, worked down at the docks and the hours were long. Some nights he wouldn't get home until 9pm when we were all tucked up in bed.

But on Fridays we could stay up and wait for Dad to come home, and he would always bring us the same thing.

"Here you go," he would say, handing us each a small square of Lindt chocolate.

"Thanks Dad!" we would say, delighted with our treat. It is funny because even now I will have a small piece of Lindt chocolate before I go to bed. Every time I taste it, it just takes me back to those Friday nights at home with my family. They were happy times.

I had a really happy childhood and I was close to both my brother and my sister. My brother looked like your typical protective big brother, but he was actually quite shy, and I had a very close bond with my sister Pat. She seemed like the older sister in some way as she was always so confident and I was more shy.

Being a mum and grandmother now, I could see why my own mum was overly protective. I had been born three months prematurely on May 1, 1947 and weighed just 3lbs 9oz. My mum, who had a normal pregnancy with Brian, had started to get pains in her tummy while pregnant with me at six months. She went to the doctors, but they didn't seem too concerned, so they sent her home again. But then she started to bleed and was taken to hospital – then I arrived!

The doctors had told my mum and dad that because I had been born so early, and I was so tiny, that I probably wouldn't make it. Hospitals didn't have the knowledge or advanced equipment to look after premature babies in the way they do today.

Mum asked for a priest to come to the hospital, and as I lay in my incubator, I was read my last rites. They really thought I wouldn't survive.

But by some miracle, I got stronger and stronger, and as time went on, I gained weight and my mum and dad were able to take me home.

Coming into the world in the way I did, and needing care from doctors and nurses, set me on a bit of a path for life. I have had a fair few health issues over the years, some I will come onto later, but as a child I was often ill, a sickly child they would say.

I remember being about five years old when I had a cyst grow on my neck. It came up like a big ball and it was all scaly in texture. My mum took me to the doctors, and she was told I had tuberculosis and it had affected the lymph nodes in my neck.

They arranged for me to have the cyst removed at a hospital in London, so my dad took me on the train.

"Bill, please be careful with her," I remember Mum saying as we left. "Don't let anyone knock into her or the cyst might burst." She was worried someone on the train would poke me with an elbow.

They removed the cyst and I would have to go back to the hospital now and then to get the area burnt. I still have a scar at the bottom left side of my neck now.

Being wrapped up in a bubble meant there were some skills in life I just never got around to learning, like swimming or learning to ride a bike.

When we were younger, we used to spend some of our summer holidays in Yorkshire. My nan lived up there and my uncle worked in a local hotel as a manager. Brian, Pat and I always used to feel so lucky as we got to spend time in the hotel, which had a huge pool.

One day, I was walking along near the deep end when someone pushed me in.

I remember the fear as my body hit the water, falling fast to the bottom, not being able to breathe. I can't remember who pulled me out, the whole experience was so traumatic, but I do know it scared the life out of me so much that it put me off ever learning to swim. Even now, if Harry and I are on holiday, I won't go into the pool or in the sea.

And while kids would ride the streets on their bikes, it was something I never got to do. I only sat on a bike for the first time a few years ago – my friend Jackie bought me a three-wheeler so I could learn. I hopped on and tried to ride on the drive, but I was very wobbly – so much so that the kids told me I couldn't be trusted on my own with it!

I suppose learning to ride a bike, you need confidence, and that isn't something I ever felt I had as a child. I was really tall and always felt like I stuck out, which I hated. My school friends were always shorter and I wished I could be the same height as them.

Pat – who was two years and five months younger than me – and I went to the local comprehensive, while Brian went to a grammar school called George Green. He was the clever one and had passed his 11-plus with flying colours. Pat and I were not as academic as Brian so we didn't even get to do the exam.

I couldn't wait to leave school. Back then you could leave early if you had a job lined up, so as soon as my 14th birthday came around, I got a job and left. I remember there was a girl in my class who was born two days before me on April 29 and she wasn't allowed to leave as she didn't have a job, so she had to stay until the summer. I started working at a hair salon in Barking, not far from our house, called Rayners. It was owned by a lady called Alice and her sisters Brenda and Joan worked there too. It turned out to be a right family affair, as a couple of years later, Pat joined the salon as a Saturday girl. My sister had no intention of getting into hairdressing, but she came in to help out one weekend and ended up doing an apprenticeship and staying on.

I absolutely loved my job. I loved chatting to the customers, my regulars, and exchanging bits of gossip, chatting about holidays, that sort of thing. And Alice was lovely – in fact, I am still great friends with her now.

I was working in the salon when I met Harry. I remember introducing him to my parents for the first time.

"He looks like a smart boy," my mum told me. "His suit is nicely pressed."

And Harry didn't just look smart, he was clean too. I remember one day he went to use the bathroom in my mum and dad's house and moments later I heard the tap running. "Oh good, he is nice and clean," I remember telling my mum. "He washes his hands after using the toilet." Harry laughs when I tell people that story, especially because it all could have ended between us if he hadn't washed his hands! But for us girls that sort of thing is important – you don't want a man with dirty hands, you don't know where they have been!

I will never forget meeting Harry's parents for the first time. His lovely mum Violet was so, so nervous. Harry hadn't brought a girlfriend home before so I think she had got herself into a bit of a panicky state before meeting me, so much so that as I walked in, I could see her little neck was all red and blotchy.

I remember her bringing me a cup of tea, her hands a bit shaky with nerves. I smiled before taking a sip. It tasted funny, like it was off. I glanced into the kitchen and saw a bottle of sterilised milk on the side. I hated sterilised milk, but I didn't have the heart to tell her – and even years down the line, whenever she would offer me a cup of tea, I would just tell her, "I am okay thanks, Mum."

I called Harry's parents Mum and Dad, and Harry did the same with mine. It was a sign of respect and I had huge respect for Harry's parents.

Harry's mum was one of the nicest people you could ever meet. She was always on the go. She worked in a cake factory and the local Co-Op – I remember her working in a sugar factory at one point too – and when she was back at home she was cleaning the communal stairways and the lift.

I remember Harry Sr was very shy. He loved boxing and football and being around the men, but he didn't seem as comfortable around women. He was always so lovely to me, but you could always tell he held back a little around women. Harry was exactly the same, so when Harry plucked up the courage to ask me to marry him, I couldn't believe it.

Chapter 4

Popping the question

'I asked Sandra's dad for her hand in marriage. Was I nervous? Yeah, I guess I was a bit – find me a man who isn't when he proposes'

Harry

I am not a very romantic person, so our engagement wasn't anything too fancy. Sandra knows I love her dearly, she is my life, but I am not one for kissing, cuddling or holding hands in public. No way, it is just not a bit of me. She always says I don't really show my feelings or emotions – apart from when I saw her in the jungle and I cried like a baby! But I show Sandra how much she means to me in other ways, and she knows she means the world to me, even if I don't say it that often.

For example, every Christmas I will pretend I haven't bought her anything, it is a joke I use every year and it doesn't get old.

"Oh Sandra, I am sorry, I ran out of time and forgot to get you anything," I'll tell her, pulling a cheeky grin behind her back.

I'll spend all of Christmas Day apologising for forgetting her present, and then I will surprise her later in the day when she least expects it with some clothes or jewellery.

One year I put her Christmas present under her pillow and another year I bought her a diamond ring. I couldn't tell you what I paid for it, but I thought it would be a good idea to put it in a Christmas cracker.

"Oh my goodness, look at this ring," she said as the yellow diamond landed on her lap. "It is so gorgeous. I can't believe this has come out of a Christmas cracker!"

"Out of a cracker? Sandra, that is your Christmas present from me!" I told her and we both started laughing.

Sandra and I had been courting for about 18 months before I proposed – not with a yellow diamond, I should say, but with a ring I could afford at the time. We had some great times together during our courtship, many of which would involve Pat and Frank.

I remember we would all go to the Lime and the Lamb in Brentwood for a basket or scampi or a prawn cocktail. Sometimes we would go to pubs further out in the country, but that would depend on how we played that day – if we lost, I would want to get out as far as possible so I didn't have to see anyone.

Popping the question

The Moby Dick was also one of our favourites. The older guys at West Ham used to go there all the time. The head waiter was called Dick – nothing to do with the pub, mind you, that was just a coincidence.

He was a good fella, Dick. Like us lot at West Ham, he was a punter, a gambler, and liked a bet or two on the horses.

He would always look after us. When we wanted to have a bit of dinner at home, we would drive to the restaurant. "Drive around the back," he would tell us. So we would go to the car park behind the restaurant and find Dick dishing out scampi and tartar sauce wrapped in cellophane straight out of the window from the kitchen. We would give him a couple of quid, but he also gave us a fair few freebies.

On nights out, everybody would get dressed up. You wouldn't see any fella not in a suit with a tie. Even if you didn't have a lot of money, the money you did have was spent on clothes. If you had 20 quid, you'd go and get a suit made.

I remember going to Phil Seagal to get fitted for a mohair, Italian suit for a night at the Blind Beggars in Whitechapel. It was always a slim fit shirt, narrow leg trousers and a tie, a skinny one. A bit like football boots, our shoes were always clean. And polished.

The girls would all go to a great effort to get dressed up, even just for a night down the local. They'd have their dresses on and their hair would be done nicely. It was what we did back then.

Sandra and I also liked to have a little weekend away down at my mum and dad's caravan in Leysdown-on-Sea in Kent. Sometimes Frank and Pat would come along. I remember me and Frank would have a kickabout, seeing who could do the most headers and keepy-uppies. I guess you could say we were trying to impress the girls, but they couldn't be less impressed. They had zero interest in football.

We would always go down to my mum and dad's caravan when I was a kid, and it was our escape out of the East End on the weekends. My dad would finish work at the docks at 6pm and then he would dash home on a Friday night. We would all get the bus from Aberfeldy Street down to Leysdown. It would take about four hours as there were no motorways then. We would have a little stop for a cup of tea at the half-way house for 45 minutes and then we would go on with our journey. As soon as we got down there, Mum would be in the caravan putting the kettle on and Dad would go off to the fish and chip shop.

Sandra loved it when I took her down there. We would go to this little café where they'd serve up roast dinners, or we would get fresh fish and chips. Years later we would take Mark and Jamie down there, and they loved it too. Sometimes they would spend the whole six weeks of the summer school holidays down there with my mum and dad and wouldn't want to come back home.

Popping the question

I loved spending time with Sandra. I had never taken a girl home before to meet my mum and dad, Sandra was the first. To be honest, I had never really been that serious with a girl. Before I met Sandra, I wasn't even sure if I wanted to be in a relationship or have a girlfriend. But once I set eyes on her in the Two Puddings, that was it – she was the girl I was going to marry.

I remember I asked Sandra's dad for her hand in marriage. Was I nervous? Yeah, I guess I was a bit – find me a man who isn't when he proposes – but I felt comfortable in Bill's company and comfortable enough to ask him.

I got down on one knee to propose, I remember that, but I couldn't tell you much else about the proposal – only that Sandra said 'yes'.

I didn't have a lot of money back then. Yes, I was playing for West Ham, but I was earning £20 a week. It certainly wasn't enough for us to get engaged, let alone get married and buy a house.

I ended up getting a job loading up the shelves in Mr Wilson's Supermarket on Green Street, which was opposite Upton Park station, just to earn some extra cash.

Mr Wilson was a Geordie and I got on with him well. He was a big football fan, a really nice fella.

"I need a job," I told him one day. "I want to get married and I can't afford it on my wages."

"Do you fancy stacking some shelves for me?" he asked. "You can start on Monday." And so I did.

It was pretty normal for footballers to have a regular job on the side back then – they'd get jobs in the summer to keep a bit of cash coming in. I remember the late, great Bobby Moore worked in a factory in Barking. Frank Snr and John Bond also both coached in a local school for £2.50 for three or four hours a day. The manager thought it would be good for them to learn and have that skill and it was good to have the extra cash.

Sandra was good at saving, much better than me. To be fair, she probably saved more for the wedding than I did. She was earning £13 a week and if we were 20p short in our savings, it was Sandra who would put it in.

I saved a bit from football and my supermarket job, but I used to like a bet. I would often go dog racing with the other players. We were all gamblers to be honest, I grew up with the culture of it.

Sandra and I managed to pull together enough money to have an engagement party down at the Loxford Club, a working men's club on Ilford High Road. Sandra's dad was a member, so we got good rates. It was quite a basic do, again nothing too fancy, and our mums did the buffet of salmon and cucumber sandwiches.

We had both sides of the family there, Frank was there with Pat, and the rest of the boys from West Ham. I think Sandra's mates were in their element as they were all West Ham fans!

Popping the question

As our wedding day was approaching, I needed a best man. Luckily I wasn't short on good mates being in a football team, but there was only one man for the job. Frank.

Unfortunately, just a few weeks before we were due to get married, Frank was involved in a horror tackle on the pitch. In truth, it is probably one of the worst I have ever seen.

Willie Carlin, a midfielder at Sheffield United, went over the top on Frank and took him right out. It was absolutely terrible and Frank's leg was wrecked. He was only 18 and just five months into his playing career. I think he – and the rest of us – thought his playing career was over before it had even started.

But one thing I can tell you about Frank is that he never gives up and he did everything to come back from that injury. I remember how he would run up and down the terraces at Upton Park to build up his leg muscles and get his strength and fitness back.

Sadly, not before our wedding, though, as Frank arrived on crutches. We laughed about it afterwards, of course, and if you look at our wedding pictures, there is Frank with a massive cast on his leg. I even signed it for him.

It is a day Sandra and I won't forget – and I am sure Frank won't for other reasons!

Chapter 5

Wedding bells

'Our honeymoon in Torquay
turned out like an episode of
Only Fools and Horses'

Sandra

Like most little girls, I had always dreamed of my wedding day. Growing up, my sister Pat and I would always talk about getting married, wondering what sort of weddings we would have and the dresses we would wear. Harry and I got married on June 30, 1968. It was a beautiful day, not a cloud in the sky.

I remember I couldn't wait to get into my dress. I got it months earlier during a shopping trip with my sister, Pat, and my mum. I was quite fussy and the dress needed to be right.

"I am not sure about any of these," I told them, going through the racks. "None of them feel right."

"You'll find the perfect dress," my mum told me.

"This one is lovely, but it is just far too expensive," I said as I took the dress by its skirt to take a closer look.

"You could always hire it," the assistant said. "You get more for your money if you hire the dress."

"I absolutely love this one," I told them as I ran my fingers over the material. "This is the one." It was beautiful and had little crystal droplets on it.

The thought of hiring my wedding dress didn't actually worry me. After all, you only ever wear it once and then it spends the rest of its life in a box up in the loft.

On the morning of the wedding, I was feeling a little nervous. I remember taking a deep breath and telling myself, "Come on, you can do this."

To be honest, the thing that was most worrying me was Harry being late. It is traditionally the bride who keeps her groom waiting, but I hate being late for anything. Even now, if Harry and I are going out for dinner with friends and we are the last couple to arrive and everybody else is sitting down at the table, I get all hot and red. I find it so embarrassing. Harry, on the other hand, is a last-minute man. He will sit around to the very last moment and then rush upstairs to get ready with seconds to spare. So when

I arrived at St Margaret's Church in Barking, I was very relieved to see he did make it on time.

My dad walked me down the aisle to the *Wedding March*. Pat was my bridesmaid and she wore a dress with a claret underskirt and a pale blue top. They were West Ham colours, but it wasn't meant to be as blatant as that, just a little nod to the team. My cousin Susan, who was about five at the time, and Harry's two other cousins were also bridesmaids.

My brother Brian, who got married a year earlier, was Harry's best man and Frank, my soon-to-be-brother-in-law, was there on his crutches.

It wasn't a showbiz wedding, not like the big celebrity weddings you see today. There were a few West Ham players there, maybe a few fans outside the church and a couple of photographers for the newspapers, but that was it.

We had a wonderful wedding day with a lovely reception upstairs at the Loxford Club where we had our engagement party months earlier. I remember we danced to Frank Sinatra's *Strangers in the Night*. However, mine and Harry's song is Billy Joel's *Just The Way You Are*, and I am pretty sure we got through it without Harry treading on my toes!

We had a sit-down meal and that night we had a buffet with yellow legs with pepper and vinegar, and jellied eels, Harry's favourite.

Wedding bells

After such a lovely day with family and friends, Harry and I were looking forward to getting away for a few days, just the two of us, for our honeymoon in Torquay. But instead of it being a relaxing holiday, it turned out to be like an episode of *Only Fools and Horses* from start to finish, with Harry in the starring role as Del Boy!

It all started on our journey down. A few months before the wedding, Harry had bought a bright red Jaguar from one of the other players at West Ham, John Bond, for £200, which was a lot of money back then. And you can probably guess what happened next... An hour or so into our journey and the car breaks down; the head gasket had completely gone.

"I can't believe it," Harry said, putting his hands through his hair. "This is meant to be in good nick, it is only a couple of years old."

It later turned out the car was two years older than Harry had thought, so wasn't in that good nick!

It took us more than eight hours to get down to Torquay in the end, including all the stops we made for Harry to fill the car up with water.

"This honeymoon is a disaster," we agreed when we finally got to our hotel.

We had been recommended the hotel and when Harry booked it, the owner spoke directly to Harry on the phone.

"When you and Sandra are down here, why don't you invite a few of your football friends over for dinner one evening. As my guests, it will be on me," he said.

Harry decided to ask John Bonham, who he had played with at West Ham but had since moved down to Torquay, and another player, Bill Kitchener. They both arrived with their wives and we all had a lovely meal, lots of wine. At the end of the night, Harry was handed the bill.

"Thank you, but the owner said this one is on him," Harry explained. "We agreed to it when I booked it."

"I am sorry," the waiter replied, looking confused. "The owner is now on holiday in Spain and won't be back for a few weeks. I am very sorry, but I don't know anything about this."

"Oh great," I thought. "We've got no money and we now have to pay this bill! This is another nightmare."

The journey home wasn't much better – we broke down again and it took us another eight hours to get home.

But our honeymoon wasn't our first disastrous holiday. The year before we got married, we went for a week away with Frank and Pat, my friend Joy from school and her husband Roger Cross, who by coincidence was also at West Ham with Harry and Frank.

"Let's all get away for a week," Harry said.

"But we can't really afford it, Harry," I told him.

"Come on, it will be okay," he reassured me. "Let's just go and enjoy ourselves, it will be fine."

Wedding bells

It was May time, and Harry and the boys had just finished the season. The weather was roasting hot for that time of year, and Harry had booked us a place in Bournemouth. We couldn't get into the same guesthouse as Frank and Pat and Roger and Joy, as it was fully booked, but we weren't far away.

I remember it being beautiful when we arrived, the sun was shining and even though the town was booked up, the beaches were empty as the kids were still at school. We finally got to the place Harry had booked, Treetops I think it was called.

"Here are your rooms," the man said, pointing at two garden sheds.

"Our rooms? No, sorry Sir, I think there has been a mistake," Harry said.

"I am sorry, the main house is full and this is all I have got," the owner shrugged.

I could tell Harry was annoyed. We opened the doors to these little wooden huts and found a camp bed laid out in each.

"Harry, I have got a load of tools in my shed," I said, horrified.

"Tools?" Harry asked, "I have got a bloody lawnmower!"

That night, Harry and I slept in our separate garden sheds. I didn't get a wink of sleep and Harry didn't either.

"Come on, why don't we get out of here," Harry told me the next morning. "I'll go and sort the bill and get the car ready," Harry said.

We were about 10 minutes down the road and Harry turned to me and said, "Now don't have a go Sarn, but I haven't paid the bill."

"What!?" I said, my voice slightly raised. "No Harry, please tell me you are joking?"

"I am not paying for that, it is absolutely diabolical what they did to us," Harry said, shaking his head.

"Why didn't you tell me you weren't going to pay the bill?" I asked.

"Because you would have had a heart attack!" he replied.

And he was right, I would have gone mad at him had he told me. I was quite cross with him now. We could have got into huge trouble, and I have always been one to pay my way. But the thought of not sleeping next to a shovel that night made me feel better.

We drove down to where the others were staying. They had a guest house – not a shed! – with Frank and Roger upstairs and Pat and Joy downstairs.

"I don't suppose our friends could come and join us?" Frank asked the owner.

Minutes later, he was putting an extra bed upstairs for Harry and one in the girls' room for me.

That night as I got into bed, glad not to be sleeping in a shed, I wondered to myself, 'What have I done?' Taking a deep breath and closing my eyes, I thought to myself, 'This is another nice mess you've got me into, Harry!'

And I suppose that 'another mess' has become a bit of a regular saying in our marriage. I call Harry Mr Pastry because he is so clumsy, just like that old 1950s children's TV character. For example, he can't make a cup of tea without knocking over the sugar bowl or dripping tea all over the work surface. There was one time when he was jet washing the drive and thought it would be a good idea to water my plants at the same time. I just remember watching in horror from the kitchen as all of their heads went flying off everywhere! His jet washed drive was covered in flower heads. Not only does Harry like to make a mess, but he has certainly got me into a mess or two over the years!

Chapter 6

'Mad' house

'It is now three o'clock in the morning and I am driving around Barking looking for the dog'

Harry

"You've paid £6,200 for a house, you're both mad." That was my dad's reaction when we told him we had bought our first house in Barking.

"But Dad, it is a really nice house. Plus, it is good to own your own house these days," I tried to reason, but he wasn't having any of it. "You should have got yourself on the council list, you're wasting your money," he told us. My dad couldn't make sense of it. Why would we pay that much money for a house, when we could rent off the council for a few quid a week.

But Sandra and I had always talked about buying a house once we were married, and much like we did for the wedding, Sandra and I had saved for a long time for our first home.

My dad didn't see the sense in spending all that money on a house, but then growing up on a council estate was all he ever knew.

My dad had a tough upbringing, a very hard life. I never knew my grandparents – his mum died and his dad wasn't a nice bloke. I don't know anything about him really as my dad never spoke about him, but people in the East End would tell me how he used to beat my nan up and all sorts.

"Your grandad was the most evil bloke, a horrible man," one of them said to me one day.

I heard one story about how my nan had been hop picking down in Kent and when she came back home a few days later than expected, he dragged her off the lorry and he beat her up. He kicked her, booted her in the street, and ended up breaking her leg. Her friends ended up putting her in a wheelbarrow to take her to hospital. He was a very nasty man by all accounts, so I don't blame my dad for one second for not wanting to know him.

My dad had a sister, Frarnie; she is still alive and came to visit us a couple of Christmases ago. And then there was George, my dad's twin brother; he died about two years ago. My dad told me a story about when they both went to Susan Lawrence Primary School on Ricardo Street – the same school I went to many years later – and they were so poor he and George had to share plimsolls. They would take it in turns to play games, because they couldn't afford two pairs.

My dad and his siblings never had the chance to be a family in the way that my kids and I know. When my nan died, all the kids got farmed out to different families and care homes. They were split up and fostered by different families. My dad lived with the Cabana family. They were a big family and had two boys, Archie and Harry, and they would all play football together. They grew up as brothers, really. My dad was a good footballer. I don't doubt that if things had worked out differently for him that he would have been a professional player; he was that good. He definitely would have been able to afford his own house.

The place Sandra and I ended up buying was not too far from her parents' house, and her brother Brian and his wife lived just around the corner. Sandra's whole family were in Barking, her aunts, her uncles, her nan – they all lived in terraced houses within one or two miles of each other.

It wasn't uncommon for footballers to live in a terraced or semi-detached house back then. Bobby Moore lived with his wife, Tina, in Chigwell, which we all thought was the best area to live in, but he was the only footballer I knew who lived in a detached house.

Amazing players like Geoff Hurst or Martin Peters didn't even live in detached houses then. They all lived on a little estate near Hornchurch in houses that cost around four grand each.

"This place is incredible," I said to Bobby one day. His house was the biggest and best house I had ever seen. About six months ago I was around that way in Essex and I drove past his old house. I couldn't believe it, it looked like a little doll's house, honestly it was tiny, and I don't mean that disrespectfully to anyone, but back then we thought he was living in a mansion.

Bobby was not only one of the greatest defenders of all time, but one of the greatest footballers. He was also a very close and dear friend.

I first met Bobby when I was called up to the first team squad in 1965 and he had been made the England captain. He was only in his early 20s with this huge responsibility on his shoulders, but he took it on with so much ease. It was incredible, really.

But he always made time for everyone. He was a very popular player on and off the pitch, he was well liked and everyone wanted to be his friend. I was lucky to call him a friend. Bobby was just a normal fella. He might have been the England captain, the only one in history to achieve what he did by bringing home the World Cup, but he didn't have the same limelight and pressure that players like Bobby would have today. Put it this way, he might have had the same level of fame as David Beckham if he walked down the street, but he certainly didn't have the same money or attention.

I remember him telling me how they all got a grand each for winning the World Cup. One of the greatest footballing achievements ever for an English team, even to this day, and they all walked away with a grand. A grand!

He told me how the night they won, the players were invited to a big function to celebrate, but the wives weren't allowed in. Don't ask me why, but I just remember him telling me how they all had to wait in the lobby of the hotel. Anyway, this function goes on for hours, so in the end, Bobby left, and he and Tina and some of the other players and their wives ended up going to Daniel Le Roux's club. They were shown to their table and it was right next to the toilet – the worst table in the house. Bobby was the England captain and they had won the World Cup that afternoon, and they stuck him next to the toilet. It is quite unbelievable when you think about it.

But Bobby would never have moaned. We were all equal back then. We all came from working class backgrounds and no one was better than anyone else and no one was judged on how big their house was.

When Sandra and I moved into our house, the first thing we wanted to do was to get a dog. We had spoken about starting a family, but we had also always wanted a Boxer.

We were really keen to get a puppy and I was told there was a good breeder out in Essex. Better still, this breeder is so brilliant I was told, that his Boxers don't slobber, and anyone who has had a Boxer knows they can be slobbery dogs.

'Brilliant,' I thought. 'I'll get us a little puppy Boxer from this bloke out in Essex and he is not going to be dribbling all over us.'

So one Sunday I drove out to meet this top breeder. "I haven't got any puppies," he told me when I got there. I had driven all this way for a dog, and Sandra had bought dog food and toys, so I thought I better go home with one.

In the end, I picked a beautiful looking dog, who we called Matty. He is a proper dog, a year old so no longer a puppy, but what harm can he do, I thought.

Well, I only had him a day and he chewed the telephone table that we were given as a wedding present. He would chew anything and everything. Our letterbox was at the bottom of the door and he loved to chew the post. That Christmas, he chewed all of our Christmas cards so that we couldn't see who they were from.

One day, after another chewing episode, I tapped Matty on the nose. I didn't hit him, I would never do that, but I gave him a little tap to say what he was doing was naughty. He looked at me and started shaking. I thought, 'Oh God, I have scared him now.'

The next day we were playing Queen's Park Rangers, so before the game I took Matty for a walk and let him off the lead for a run.

A few minutes passed and he'd not come back to me. I chase after him and he just keeps running and running.

'I am never going to catch him,' I thought to myself, so I headed back home to grab my car.

It is now three o'clock in the morning and I am driving around Barking looking for Matty. 'I have only gone and lost him,' I thought. 'Sandra is going to be devastated.' All of a sudden, out of nowhere, Matty appears, two miles down the road from our house. I got him in the car and gave him a cuddle.

Eleven years we had Matty. Mark and Jamie grew up with him and they adored him as much as Sandra and I did. He was a right little scatterbrain, bloody barmy, but he was a fantastic little dog and, in many ways, like our first baby.

Chapter 7

A new arrival

'We couldn't shake that feeling of worry and spent those early weeks terrified'

Sandra

"I'm pregnant!" I told Harry in the summer of 1969. We were both thrilled to be expecting a baby, but we were also feeling nervous.

Just five months earlier, I had said those same two words to Harry.

"I'm pregnant!" I said as a huge smile appeared on his face.

"No, what? Are you really? You're joking!" he said.

"I'm not!" I told him. "We are having a baby!" I smiled as he put his arms around me, squeezing me tightly. It felt like a very exciting time for us. We had been married for a year, we were in our new home and we couldn't wait to become parents.

But then, when I was around 12 weeks pregnant, I sadly suffered a miscarriage. I remember that day so vividly. It was February 1969. I had been working at the hairdressers and it had been snowing all day. By the time I came to leave that evening, there were no buses in Barking due to bad weather, so I ended up walking back in the thick snow. My feet were freezing and I couldn't feel my hands. I had already started to feel a bit unwell – weak and slightly dizzy. I couldn't wait to get back home in the warmth. But by the time I walked through the front door, I realised I had lost our baby.

Harry was playing away at Mansfield in the fifth round of the FA Cup. They lost 3-0. Of course, there were no mobile phones so there was no way for me to contact him; I had to wait for him to come home to tell him we had lost the baby. It was heartbreaking.

It wasn't a great time for either of us and I cried a lot.

So when I fell pregnant that July, I couldn't believe it – and neither could Harry.

We were over the moon to be expecting again and felt very lucky. But we couldn't shake that feeling of worry and spent those early weeks terrified the same thing could happen again. It also didn't help that I was suffering very badly with morning sickness.

In fact, I was sick throughout the whole nine months and even during labour.

I remember at Christmas, when I was about five months pregnant, I had to go into hospital to be put on a drip, it was that bad. I felt awful. Then nearer to the end of the pregnancy, doctors told me Mark was breech and I might need a C-section.

"I am fed up with being pregnant," I said to Harry as my due date approached.

"You'll be okay, Sarn," Harry reassured me. "There is not that long to go now."

I felt guilty for feeling so miserable after everything I had been through with the miscarriage, but I wasn't enjoying my pregnancy.

I ended up being two weeks overdue and those two weeks felt like they went on forever.

I remember finally going into labour – Mark had turned by this point, thankfully, and things finally started to get going. I had gas and air to help with the pain, though I could still feel a lot of it so I am sure they didn't switch it on! Then, finally a fortnight after his due date, at 8.40pm on April 16, 1970, Mark James Redknapp was born and suddenly all of those feelings of sickness just disappeared.

He was a gorgeous baby, so handsome, with a mop of dark hair, and I fell in love with him as soon as I saw him. When you are pregnant you think about who your baby might look like and I didn't imagine that he would have so much hair.

Back then, the baby was taken to the creche and cared for by the nurses. It was wonderful as it meant you could get a decent night's sleep. Every morning, when the nurses brought Mark to me, he would have a different hairstyle. As a hairdresser, I found it so funny. "Here he is, Mr Redknapp," one nurse said, as she brought Mark in with a side parting.

Harry wasn't at the birth. In those days, if your wife went into labour and you were training or you had a match, you went to training or played the match. The governor would get a phone call and the player would be told at half-time or after the match that their baby had been born.

I remember Harry telling me about one player who wasn't going to play because his wife was having a baby and there was uproar in the team. It was totally unheard of.

Harry worshipped Mark. He would take him everywhere. He would put him in the car, drive him around, he loved being with Mark. Harry's never changed a nappy in his life – not for Mark or Jamie or the grandchildren – he wouldn't know where to start and he would probably only make a mess. But that was what the men did, they went to work, they came home and their wives looked after the children and the home.

In many ways, me and the boys were lucky that Harry was playing football. It meant he would go to training a couple of times a week, play at a weekend and then he would still have time to play with the boys while they were still young. He would often go and pick them up from school – he was usually late! – but that was a nice thing he got to do and it was nice for the boys.

And that didn't change when Harry became a manager. Obviously the boys were getting older by then, but Harry was still around in the week.

I remember waiting for Harry to come home from matches and wondering what mood he would be in. If they lost the game, I would make sure the boys were out of the way and didn't say the wrong thing to him. I would tell the boys to go and put a film on in their room. But if they won, Harry would come home delighted and go for a kickabout with the boys in the garden.

There were great things about being the wife of a footballer, and then manager. We are very lucky that we live in a nice house and eat out at nice places. But there were a lot of downsides, too.

Chapter 8

On the move

'It was a new Georgian townhouse and it was £16 a month. It was a beautiful area; it had fishing lakes, the beach; we were really lucky'

Harry

Sandra and I were about to make a huge decision that would change our lives forever. It was the 1970-71 season and I knew my time at West Ham was well and truly done when I had a huge fallout with manager Ron Greenwood. We were on a run of bad form, only winning one game, and my relationship with Ron had hit an all-time low. We were playing Newcastle at home when we went 1-0 down. I thought I was playing alright that day, probably the only one, so when Ron took me off for Trevor Brooking, I was absolutely furious, and I let him know it as well. Instead of running off the pitch like you are supposed to, I made sure I took my time and walked. Slowly.

After the game, which we ended up losing 2-0, Ron came into the dressing room to give me a dressing down.

"Don't you ever do that to me again," he fumed. "If I take you off the pitch, you run off, you don't walk!"

I was furious. "And don't do that to me. Why is it always me you take off?"

As he stormed off, I spotted a crate of beer next to me. Bobby Moore and Jimmy Greaves were just about to crack one open when I picked one up and lobbed it across the room. It hit the wall and smashed, beer and glass everywhere.

I ended up finishing the season. West Ham finished 20th, which was three places down on the previous season, and we narrowly avoided relegation from the First Division by just seven points. I went on to play 22 league games in the '71-72 season and then that was it for me. After 175 games for West Ham, seven seasons and eight goals, I was done.

In early August 1972, I signed for Bournemouth. John Bond, who was just ending his footballing career at West Ham as I was starting mine, had taken over as manager. He was a top, top player and I admired him greatly. He was the one who sold me that dodgy Jaguar that broke down on the way to our honeymoon in Torquay.

John's assistant was Kenny Brown, who had also played at West Ham for many years. On the same day, John signed former Everton player Jimmy Gabriel, who had moved to Southampton. He also signed Bobby Howe, my West Ham team-mate who I played with in the FA Youth Cup final.

In truth, the decision to move to Bournemouth was probably easier for me than it was for Sandra, but it was still a big move.

We had lived in Barking together for about five or six years by this point, all in close proximity to Sandra's family. It had been the perfect location for us as it was in between Upton Park and the training ground, and it was close to where Sandra worked in the hairdressers. Now we were moving miles away from her parents and the rest of her family, all of whom she was really close to. Sandra had just fallen pregnant with Jamie, and Mark was still a toddler. It was going to be hard for her to be away.

The journey back to London was also a long one. There was no motorway, so it would take more than four hours to get there. The drive was always a bit of a schlep.

Sandra and I ended up renting a little house from the club. It was a new Georgian townhouse on the Riverslea estate and it was £16 a month. It was a beautiful area; it had fishing lakes, the beach; we were really lucky.

The move was made easier by the fact that I knew John and Kenny and had played with Bobby, who also moved onto the Riverslea estate with his wife and daughter Kimberley.

Jimmy, his wife and three daughters, also rented a house there, which faced ours. We all had in common that we were away from home. We had to share a car together to training every day, and we used to drink in a nice little pub around the corner called the Ship in Distress. We nicknamed it the QE2 and it was an old smugglers' pub back in the day, they reckon.

Bournemouth felt like a good club to be at. There were a lot of players coming in at that time, and it was going places. The chairman, Mr. Harold Walker, was a wealthy guy, a very nice man, and he was putting a lot of money into it.

After a couple of years, Sandra and I decided to sell our house in Barking and buy our Georgian in Bournemouth.

There wasn't money in the property market in those days. People weren't into buying or selling houses to make money.

The club secretary, who ran that side of things, told me they were looking to sell the houses off.

"We are very interested," I told him. "We love it down here, so we would love to buy one if we can."

"Okay Harry," he said. "I'll get a price for you."

A few days later, he called me up. "Harry, I have got a price on your three-bedroom house, it is going to cost you £15,000."

"Yeah okay, we will take it," I said with a smile. We didn't live in a three-bedroom, we were in a four-bedroom, and that would have cost us £16,000. I didn't say anything. We saved a grand and had a result.

The following year, on June 25, 1973, Jamie was born. We gave him the middle name Frank after my mate Frank, and Jamie's uncle. We often get asked if he is a James, but he's not, he is just a Jamie, or Jim Bob, that is my nickname for him.

Some people might say women are superheroes for giving birth, and they are not wrong. I have seen horror tackles on the pitch over the years when players have been badly injured – and many others where they have had a little nick on the shin or ankle and gone down like a ton of bricks! – but Sandra has a pain barrier like I have never known. It is quite unbelievable, really.

Sandra is quite accident-prone – admittedly there was one horrific accident where I ran her over in my car and that definitely wasn't her fault, though more on that later – but when she is in pain or hurt, she never complains. She doesn't even know how badly she has hurt herself.

For example, there was the night she broke her kneecap. She was hoovering the hardwood floors with the Henry Hoover and she went flying over it. Luckily, our granddaughter Molly was there with her. Sandra didn't want any fuss, so she told Molly not to bother me and crawled upstairs and got into bed to rest her leg. The next day, Sandra woke up in absolute agony. "You're going to the hospital, Sarn, you need to get this looked at," I told her.

I drove her up to the hospital and they told her she had broken her kneecap, but not some tiny little hairline fracture, she had only gone and smashed it right across the front.

Later that day, she told me that she was in pain during the night, but wanted me to have a good night's sleep and thought she would be alright in the morning. Honestly, that is just typical Sandra.

When Mark and Jamie were born, it was no different. She didn't have the best pregnancy and labour with Mark, but Sandra didn't complain once.

It is the best feeling in the world when you become a dad. You don't ever forget it.

We didn't know we were having boys, because of course, you didn't have all the machines and scans that you have now. With Mark, we had no clue, but with Jamie we did think Sandra might be having a girl. Only because she carried him slightly differently compared to when she was pregnant with Mark and people would tell her it was definitely a girl, so much that we were then convinced. We didn't bother picking out any boys' names, but had a few picked for a girl, so when Jamie was born, it was a bit of a shock.

Sandra was an absolutely fantastic mum. She was very caring and fussed over them all the time. She did absolutely everything for them both. I wish I could say that I helped her out, but she really did do everything. I didn't change a single nappy, I wouldn't have a clue how to. We were pretty old school, so the women did everything, and my dad would have been the same when I was born.

But I can still say it is not easy raising two kids, and she might say that is why we didn't have any more. But I think we did keep them pretty disciplined. It was important for us that both Mark and Jamie had good manners and were nice to people – polite and respectful.

There are some footballers who think they have made it and don't treat people very nicely; they have a lack of respect for others and I really hate that. Some of us have been luckier than others in life to become footballers, so I hate it when I see people getting carried away and not giving their time to other people.

Some people spoil their kids rotten and they don't know they have been born. If you give them too much, they don't appreciate it in the end. Some of them want everything and get it too. They will go to a restaurant like Nobu for dinner, order whatever they want off the menu, or they will fly first class to Barbados and stay at a luxury resort like Sandy Lane at the age of four, five or six, but then what happens when they get older? What happens when they leave school, get married and get a job that doesn't pay the money to maintain that lifestyle, what do they do then? That is why it was important for Sandra and I to make sure Mark and Jamie were never spoiled.

When the boys were little, our holidays were down at my parents' caravan in Leysdown, just like when I was their age.

I remember as a young lad going down with my mum and dad for five weeks over the summer holidays. You wouldn't believe how basic it was. You'd walk into the hop huts and no one would have been in them since the last time you were there. There would be birds nests, insects, mice, the lot. You'd have a wooden base for a bed and a couple of barrels of straw, and you'd make your bed from that. You slept on pillows made from straw and it'd be scratching you all night, in your ears, everything. We would get up at six o'clock and go picking in the hop fields. It could be chucking it down with rain and really muddy, and you'd carry on picking, your hands red raw. I would earn a shilling a bushel and we would live on what we earned down there, we didn't come home with it.

I used to love running around in the fields, pinching apples off the trees, just being in the countryside and seeing the pigs, cows and chickens. It was absolutely fantastic – it was our holiday. So when you have been there and they were the holidays you were having as a kid, it makes you appreciate everything. And we really do appreciate everything we've got and we don't take anything for granted.

I even made the boys get a paper round when they were in school. It wasn't out of the ordinary and most of their mates had one. I remember Jamie was about an hour late one morning doing his round, so I have got the bloke in the shop on the phone having a go. On that occasion I thought I would help him out, so we both jumped in the car and started delivering the papers. Jamie's on one side of the road, I am on the other.

I walked up to one house and this old boy in his dressing gown opens the door. He has got the raving hump. "What time do you call this?" he says, fuming, though I don't blame him as he has been up waiting for his paper since seven o'clock. It is now half past eight.

Then he stopped, looked at me, then smiled and said, "It is Harry, isn't it? I am a Bournemouth season ticket holder. What are you doing delivering newspapers?"

He now looks confused.

"They don't pay me very much so I have had to get a part-time job as a paperboy," I told him.

"Oh no, really?" he said, and I gave him a laugh and a wave and off I went. I don't remember Jamie being late for another paper round again after that.

Chapter 9

Boys will be boys

*"Today's lessons are rubbish,
Dad,' he would say.
'Can I come training with you?'
'Of course,' Harry would tell him.
'Just don't tell your mum!"*

Sandra

Being a mum of boys was tiring, chaotic and very noisy, but I wouldn't have it any other way. Did I want a daughter? Yes, absolutely. But when my granddaughter Molly was born a week before Christmas in 1999 I felt like she fulfilled that desire I once had to have a girl. Molly and I are so very close, and I feel like she is the daughter I never had. She is very special to me. As you get older, you go through things in life, and realise that not everything is always meant to be. You learn life has a funny way of working out.

I love my two boys to pieces. Don't get me wrong, they used to drive me mad when they were younger, but they are so loving, and it has been truly wonderful for me and Harry to watch them grow up and start their own families.

Ever since I can remember, both Mark and Jamie were into football. I don't think I can recall them being without a ball or out of their football kits, only when they went to school. Football was about the only thing Jamie liked, apart from bacon. He didn't like school and he was a fussy eater growing up. I would make fish and vegetables for dinner and would watch as he pushed it around his plate. He hated baked beans and he hated potatoes, especially mashed potatoes.

"Got any bacon and chips, Mum?" he would say.

If I cooked eggs for breakfast, Mark would only eat the yolk and Jamie would pick at the whites. Trying to get them to eat properly was a challenge.

Football was always non-stop in our house while they were growing up. They'd be playing in the hallway, smashing footballs against the door, breaking my ornaments. I used to have porcelain Lladro figurines from Spain and they would get smashed. You wouldn't be able to glue them back together either as they were broken to pieces.

Mark and Jamie would play football in the house, in the garden, on the street, anywhere they could.

We also had a snooker table and I remember they would chase each other around the room with a cue. And if they ever played snooker or football with Harry, he wouldn't ever let them win.

"Oh, let them win this time, Harry," I would say.

"Absolutely not!" he would reply. "They need to learn from a young age that you don't win everything."

They were football crazy. Mark was a West Ham fan, while Jamie liked Luton. When we lived on the Riverslea estate down in Christchurch, there was a little boy called Paul who moved from Luton with his family. They were a lovely family and huge Luton Town fans. Paul was a bit older than Jamie, though the same size in height, and a bit younger than Mark. I think Jamie looked up to Paul and that is why he followed the same team. I remember Paul's dad, Alan, would take them both up to Luton to watch the games and Jamie loved it. He had the kit and posters of players Ricky Hill, Mark and Brian Stein on his wall. I think even now Jamie still has a bit of a soft spot for Luton.

Harry noticed from a very young age that they both had a talent and the physical ability to play football, but he always instilled in them that not everyone gets to become footballers. It is not that easy.

"Just because me and your uncle played, it doesn't mean you both will too," Harry used to tell them.

But actually, by 11, Jamie was signed by Tottenham. I remember there were days when I was led to believe that Jamie was at school, but actually he would be with Harry training down at Bournemouth.

"Today's lessons are rubbish, Dad," he would say. "Can I come training with you?"

"Of course," Harry would tell him. "Just don't tell your mum!"

When it got to four o'clock Harry and Jamie, in his uniform, would come through the door.

"Did you have a good day?" I would ask.

"It was okay thanks Mum," Jamie would tell me, heading to the fridge.

Only when I learned from his teachers that he wasn't great at reading or writing did I realise that he had been having football lessons with his dad!

Jamie was always the cheekier of the two, and I knew I would be in for a day of it with him when the hair in his cow's lick would stand up – I knew he was going to be a handful that day.

Jamie wasn't ever academic and didn't enjoy school. He amazes me when I watch him now on Sky Sports as a pundit. He speaks so well and uses all of these big words I don't understand, and I think, 'But you didn't really go to school! You went to training with your dad!'

As for Mark, he liked his football, but he was also a talented runner. He ran for Dorset and was once the town champion in the 100 metres.

Though there was one competition which they didn't make when he and Harry got caught in traffic on the way down and missed the race. It was probably Harry's fault – leaving it to the last minute again.

When Mark eventually left school at 16 he signed for Bournemouth, but he got a very bad ankle injury that was so bad he would never play again.

Most people would think their love of sport comes from their dad, but I am quite sporty too. I am also very competitive. I remember one year when the children were little, I put myself forward for the mum's run on sports day.

"I think you will win, Mum," they said to me.

"I hope so," I told them as I confidently made my way down to the start line. As I took off my shoes to put on my trainers, I heard this loud noise, followed by cheering.

I looked up and I was the only one on the start line. The whistle had gone and the mums were already 10 metres down the track.

I got some ribbing from the boys over that one. They have never let me live it down.

My brother and sister were also sporty. Brian was a good rugby player and my sister Pat was into running. It is strange as I was the one with the athletic figure – Pat was curvy with boobs, whereas I was a lot taller and flat-chested.

We were quite a healthy family. That is why it came as such a terrible shock when my mum died at the young age of 51.

Jamie was just six months old and we were already living in Bournemouth, miles away, when I got the call to say she had died.

My mum and dad had been getting ready to go on holiday, and my mum had gone upstairs to pack. My dad stayed downstairs making a cup of tea.

All of a sudden he heard an almighty bang. He quickly ran up the stairs and my mum was on the floor. She had already gone. It was so quick. We later found out that she had died from a brain haemorrhage, but it was totally out of the blue and without any warning. Losing a parent is horrific, but it was totally unexpected and she was so young. We were all in shock.

Me, Harry and the boys made the long and silent journey back to London. It took double the time it would take from Bournemouth now.

I won't ever forget that journey. I felt like it wasn't ever going to end. I looked out the window, thinking about my mum, worrying about how my dad would cope. For the first time since moving down here, I felt awful and so guilty about being so far from Barking.

Boys will be boys

It was just a few months after I lost my mum that Harry got a call that would take us even further away from home.

Chapter 10

Living in America

'I remember me, Sandra and the kids ended up in a motel under a motorway. I swear it was like something out of the film Psycho'

Harry

"Harry, it is absolutely fantastic over here, you have to come over and join me."

My mate Jimmy Gabriel was on the phone. He had recently gone out to America and had been given the amazing opportunity to play for the Seattle Sounders. It was 1977 and Jimmy was in his mid-to-late 30s and was coming to the end of his career. Now he had been given a brilliant opportunity to be a player/coach. Everyone was going to America to play in those days: Pelé, Franz Beckenbauer, Bobby Moore.

"I want you to come out here with me and be a player/ coach," he told me. "I am asking Bobby Hole, too."

It sounded like too good an opportunity to miss. Jimmy had told me the stadiums were selling 28,000 tickets a week and the money was better than in England. The plan was to spend six or seven months over in America playing football, then come back to England for the rest of the year.

"You're going to love it," my mate Jimmy said to me.

Living in America was like one big holiday. All of us players lived in these fantastic apartments with swimming pools. Bobby was there with Tina, Geoff Hurst and his wife Judith, and Mike England, a Welshman who captained Tottenham Hotspur, was also over there with his wife.

It was such a brilliant life, we were very lucky. The girls would go down to the lake with the kids, us boys would go training, and then we would meet them afterwards. We would have a nice barbecue and a swim in the lake. Looking back now, they were really great times. We all got along great. The kids were friends and would be swimming in the pool until six or seven o'clock at night.

Every so often, us players would go on a road trip. The fixtures were such that you would play all the games in one place on one trip, then move on to the next. So we would go to Florida and play the Tampa Bay Rowdies and Fort Lauderdale. Then we would be off to New York, where we'd play there and onto Boston in the same trip. The girls didn't ever go, they would stay at home with our families. The first away game of the season was in Hawaii. Oh, what a terrible place to have a game of football!

I will never forget the first home game we played. It was a 66,000 sell-out in an indoor stadium, and we were against the New York Cosmos with Pelé as their star player.

Unbelievable.

By this time, the boys were into football too and they loved it. Mark and Jamie were coming to football with me – I would be training on one pitch and they would be on one of the others.

We would always stop off on the way home from training and get a hamburger or pizza, or whatever they fancied. You could get anything at any time of the day in America. You would go and get your petrol and get yourself a drink and some food. We didn't have that in England then. I felt like England was about 20 years behind the States. We didn't have a McDonald's here in those days. The only place you could get something to eat in England, at 10 o'clock at night, was a fish and chip shop. In America, you had Herfy's, a build-your-own-burger restaurant. You'd go in, get your bun, your burger, then you would load it up. Mark and Jamie loved it.

"Dad, Dad, can we go to Herfy's after training? Please?" they would beg. There was nothing like it in England.

There was also a fish and chips place Sandra and I would go to. It was all you could eat. I might have been earning more than in England over there, but it still wasn't megabucks. So I would go and get fish and chips for me and Sandra, then keep going back to get some for the kids.

Neither Mark and Jamie were that academic, they both loved football and sport, but they liked school in America. They even got mild American accents at one point, and I guess you could say they were a bit Americanised. I remember Jamie was always chewing gum and would blow the biggest bubbles you had ever seen.

In school, the teachers would encourage the kids to speak in front of the class, whereas in England they never did. Perhaps that is why Jamie is so confident in front of the camera now.

And, of course, they loved the soccer camps – you didn't get those in England either. They would go and just play football all day. They absolutely loved it.

We were about to finish our season with Seattle when Jimmy got a phone call to look after a team in Phoenix. He was offered a very attractive financial deal and a five-year contract. He called me up.

"Harry, you've got to come to Phoenix with me," he said. Seattle was a better club than Phoenix, so I wasn't sure.

"Why would I go there?" I told him.

"There is a guy who is going to call you, he has seen us at Seattle and wants to offer you a deal, too."

A few days later, I got a call from this American fella.

"Hello, Harry, it is Leonard Lesser here." It was the governor Jimmy was telling me about in Phoenix.

"Listen, we have Jimmy as a manager and we want you as a coach, we need you at Phoenix," he told me. "I need you to help Jimmy bring in a team. So tell me, what sort of money are you looking for? Your salary won't be a problem."

I thought of a silly figure, then doubled it, and then he was offering me more plus a five-year deal.

"What kind of car do you drive, Harry," Len asked. "And your wife, I will get her a car too."

Sandra couldn't drive, but he got her a convertible.

So that was us, a new franchise called Phoenix Fire, and it was now down to me and Jimmy to find players.

I had a mate called Neil Hague, who had just been transferred to Darlington, in the north of England.

"Neil, it is Harry, do you want to come and play under me and Jimmy Gabriel in the States?" I asked him. "You can bring your wife, Jean, and all the family. We can sort you an apartment, it is brilliant money."

Neil was a great lad, he was a good-looking fella, loved himself a bit, you know, and he loved the good life.

"Are you winding me up?" he asked.

"I am telling you Neil, you've got to come over here, We are all over here. It is absolutely fantastic."

"I am playing at Darlington and you are asking me if I want to come to Phoenix, Arizona?"

That was it, we had him on a three-year deal and he was on his way to the States. He felt like he had won the pools. I felt good, too, as I had just done him and five other lads from back home the biggest favour of all time.

We arrived in Phoenix and they put us in the best hotel, it was out of this world. There was a big pool where the kids went swimming; we are all having the time of our lives.

The next day at training I eventually came face-to-face with the club's chief executive, Len Lesser.

"I am not sure about him," I said to my mate.

"What do you mean? Nah, he is alright Harry, don't worry." But I had a feeling. There was something about him. He was false and I didn't get a good first impression.

"He is as good as gold," Jimmy said.

We've now been in Phoenix for a week or so, and Sandra and I are looking for somewhere to buy. We had been renting a house in Seattle for the last three years, but now we've made the move to Phoenix and I am on a five-year contract, we decided to get a permanent base.

We eventually found a house we absolutely loved under Camelback Mountain. Property was so cheap there, it was crazy. It was just stunning. It had an outdoor pool and it was half the price of anything you could buy in England.

We had only been in our new, dream house for a week and we had a friendly game against Chicago.

I walked into the dressing room and the players are up in arms.

"Harry, where are our kits?"

"What do you mean?" I asked, confused. It is about half an hour before kick off, the kits should be here.

There are 12,000 fans in the stadium, there is no room for anyone else, the gates are closed and the players don't have anything to wear.

Minutes before kick-off, these boxes arrived. Goalkeeper Kieron Baker had joined us from Norwich where he had been on loan from Ipswich Town – and hadn't had a game at either club.

He was about to make his debut for us.

"What is this?" Kieron said, the look of confusion over his face as he held up his goalkeeper shirt that was identical to the rest of the team.

"Len, our keeper can't wear the same kit as the players," I told him. "He needs his own kit!"

"Harry," he replied patronisingly, "we will be the smartest team in the league, we are all going to wear the same uniform."

I still didn't have a good feeling about Len. And my instincts were proven right when during a trip to the bank a few weeks later the cashier told me I had no money in my account.

"That can't be right," I told her. "I have just been paid my first month's wages."

But it was right. I hadn't been paid.

Len was a conman. He had got six investors involved, each of them paying a couple of million dollars into this fake club and he stole the lot. We were all part of the con. Within two weeks, we were all unemployed.

I remember me, Sandra and the kids ended up in a motel under a motorway. I swear it was like something out of the film *Psycho*, but we couldn't get anything else as we had no money. Len got three years in an open prison. As for the players, well, they knew it wasn't my fault, but I felt terrible. It ruined them, really.

I heard Len had this huge office with a big picture on the wall of him with Jimmy Carter, the then President of the United States of America, shaking hands – he only put his head on someone else's body. It was unbelievable – and we were all part of it.

Chapter 11

The C-word

'I had put off going to the doctors, but after a couple of weeks, I thought I had better get myself checked out'

Sandra

Everything came crashing down around us when we came back from America. We were back in Bournemouth, with two young boys, with no home and no jobs. Harry was feeling low and in some ways blamed himself. Of course, it wasn't his fault at all, it was all a big con, but I think he felt like he'd let us down in some way, though he hadn't. He questioned himself and wondered why he didn't see it coming. Was it all too good to be true? But I told him he couldn't possibly have known; none of us did.

The C-word

We loved our time in America, the boys had the best of both worlds by spending time over there and then coming back to see their friends in England. I enjoyed being with the other wives and grew close to Bobby's wife Tina and Geoff's wife Judith. We felt so lucky to be living our lives in America. And Harry was happy, and when Harry is happy I am too. We had even considered a permanent move because we loved it there so much, but it just wasn't meant to be.

"What am I going to do, Sarn?" Harry said, hands through his hair. I could tell he was frustrated.

"Something will come up," I reassured him. There have been many times throughout our marriage where I have told Harry things will be okay. I am quite a positive person, and I always think that what doesn't kill you makes you stronger. I'm not one of those people who dwell on things when they go wrong, I just think it was meant to happen that way. But for the first time, I felt worried too. It was a tough and scary time for us. Harry hated not working. He had worked his whole life from picking hops with his nan to working in a supermarket, stacking shelves while at West Ham.

Throughout his whole career, his low points have always been when he was out of work. Football is all he has ever known, and the thought of trying something else terrified him. "I can't read and I can't write," he would say to me. "I don't do electrics, I am not a builder, I don't have a trade under my belt."

But then one day he had a brainwave. "I have got it Sarn," he said to me, looking happier than I had seen him in weeks. "I am going to become a Bournemouth taxi driver to help us get back on our feet."

But it was no good, and Harry's dream of a quick fix was shot back down. The taxi was between £13,000 and £15,000 and we didn't have that kind of money. We didn't even have £1,500. And the banks wouldn't lend you that kind of money back then.

Harry started selling cars out of newspapers, but half of them didn't start. I remember one day having to push a car up a hill just to get it going – and I did!

Then we had a stroke of luck. Our former window cleaner, who everyone called Mad Mick, offered us his council house in Mudeford. He was a lovely man with a nice family, and he was willing to move out so we could rent it from him.

"You've saved us," Harry said.

"No, no, Harry, you are doing me a favour," he replied. Mad Mick was also down on his luck and needed to rent out his property.

I returned to hairdressing for a while to help bring in some extra cash. But instead of working in a salon, I was mobile and I would walk around the town with my huge hair hood visiting customers. I would charge set and dry for £1.50 and I would save every single penny we had. Harry was then offered a coaching role with Dave Webb at Bournemouth.

"The money isn't great," he told me. "It is only £90 a week."

"But it is a job at the end of the day, Harry, we need the money," I told him, so he took it and we tried to make ends meet.

However, things were about to get a lot worse than our financial worries. I had been bleeding and in pain on and off for a few weeks. I had put off going to the doctors, putting it down to worry and stress, but after a couple of weeks, I thought I had better get myself checked out.

"You are absolutely fine, Mrs Redknapp," the doctor assured me after an examination. "You can walk out of here and go and enjoy your life."

Relieved, I left the doctors. 'I knew I shouldn't have bothered going,' I thought to myself. 'I am fine.'

Life carried on as usual, the boys were both in school and we were getting by. But the bleeding didn't stop.

"You should go and see a specialist, Sarn," Harry said to me.

"The doctor said I am fine," I told him.

"But it's just not right, Sarn, just go back and see someone else this time," he said.

Harry has always been a worrier and always makes sure I am okay.

"Alright," I told him. "I'll go back."

A few days later, I had seen a doctor and been referred to a specialist.

"Mrs Redknapp, I would like you to come in for surgery," the specialist said when he called me one afternoon.

"Surgery?" I asked. "What for?"

"The tests have shown you have some growths on your ovaries, they are possibly cysts and we would like to remove them," he replied.

It was just days before Christmas and there was no way I was going to leave Harry and the boys to have an operation, and then spend the festive period recovering.

"Can I come after Christmas?" I asked. The sigh he gave told me that he didn't want me to wait, but he reluctantly agreed. "Okay, Mrs Redknapp, but at least let us book you in for the New Year."

I will never forget my surgery date, it was February 14, Valentine's Day.

"What a romantic way to spend today," I joked to Harry as he drove me to the hospital, trying to break the tension. I could tell Harry was nervous for me.

"They are just some cysts," I told him. "They will be gone soon."

When we arrived at the hospital, it wasn't long before I was being prepped for surgery.

A nurse took my left hand and looked at my wedding ring.

"You won't be able to take this into surgery," she said sympathetically.

"I can't take it off," I told her. "I have never taken it off." Even now, after more than 50 years of marriage, I haven't ever taken off my wedding ring.

"I'll get some tape," she said with a smile.

The surgery went well, they removed the growths, the fallopian tube and ovary – a necessity the specialist told me.

I was just glad it was over and I could carry on with life as normal with no bleeding or pain.

A month or so later, I went for a check-up.

"So Mrs Redknapp, the growths we removed were isolated, which means they were unable to penetrate any tissue or organs."

A moment or two passed. "What do you mean?" I asked him.

"They were very early stages of cancer, but it was all contained and we have removed the growths and the ovary."

I couldn't believe what I was hearing. It was the first time I was hearing the C-word. My mouth was wide open.

"Really, Mrs Redknapp, you are going to be okay," the specialist told me as he took in my reaction.

It took a while for it all to sink in, but I counted my blessings that it had all been taken away and that it had been caught early.

But then months after recovering, I started to have problems again and the bleeding returned.

"I think the best option is a full hysterectomy," the specialist told me. And that was it. Within weeks, I was back at the hospital, but this time having everything removed.

Nowadays, if a lady has a hysterectomy they are offered counselling for the trauma, but there was no such thing back then. I was warned the menopause would kick in, so I was given hormone replacement therapy to level out and balance my hormones.

It took a while to get it right – there were days when I felt like I could have committed a murder but other times, I was absolutely fine. I was on HRT for 15 years. After that time I was told that taking it for any longer would come with risks, so I should gradually reduce it. But I just came straight off them, and I was very lucky that I felt okay and had no side effects. And during the whole time I was on HRT and after, even to this day, I have never had a hot flush or sweats. I feel very lucky as I have friends who went through a terrible experience with the menopause.

After my surgery, things started to settle down. Harry was offered the chance to become caretaker manager.

"You won't believe it Sarn," he told me excitedly, "They want me to take the game against Lincoln this weekend."

Finally, things were starting to look up for us again.

Chapter 12

Tragedy strikes

'I soon drifted off. The next thing I remember, I am lying in a hospital bed. Apparently we had got onto a dangerous road, quite notorious for accidents...'

Harry

I woke up in a hospital in Rome, covered in bruises and bandages.

"What has happened?" I asked, feeling frightened and confused.

"You've been in an accident, Harry," the nurse told me. "You are lucky to be alive."

The night before I had been at an Italy versus Republic of Ireland match with my boss, the managing director of Bournemouth Brian Tiler, Michael Sinclair, the chairman of

York City, his son Adam, and Fred Whitehouse, the chairman of Aston Villa. It was the quarter-finals of the 1990 World Cup and we were in Rome to watch Ireland lose 1-0. We had been lucky enough to get tickets to see all of the games, right up until the final, and we were enjoying our summer break in Italy. We had a gorgeous hotel in San Felice and the weather was roasting hot.

'This is the life,' I thought to myself.

Brian was a fantastic guy, a real diamond of a man, and I really enjoyed his company. He came in at Bournemouth as the managing director and made me the manager. Not straight away, though. When I was caretaker manager after David Webb, a new owner came in and wanted to bring in his own manager, which turned out to be Don Megson. He was a nice guy, but it wasn't the right decision as Anton Johnson soon found out. They were losing games and Anton wasn't happy, and there was a bit of a falling out.

Eventually, I was made manager and finally had a contract.

Brian was the type of person who could read me. If I had the hump with the chairman one day or if I was feeling down because we had lost a game, he would know exactly what to do to pick me up again. He was a bit like Sandra in that way – I can count on one hand how many people in my life can make me feel better on a down day.

He just knew me inside and out.

Tragedy strikes

"Come on Harry, get your coat," he said after one loss.

"Why, where are we going, Brian?" I replied.

"We are off to Ascot Races, and we are going to forget about everything and enjoy ourselves." He was such a positive person and I loved that about him.

We loved travelling around Italy in our little people carrier. We all picked a seat on the first day and we would always sit in the same seat. Mine was near the window, which I appreciated in the hot weather.

After the Italy game, we left the stadium a bit early to avoid the crowds. As we were walking out, I came across a group of Irish fans near a pizza place.

"Harry!" they shouted. "How are you?"

I went over to them and they told me they couldn't get tickets for the game.

"You are so lucky," they told me. "We've been watching the game from out here."

We were chatting away about the game – they were in good spirits considering their national team had just lost the quarter-final of a World Cup – when I heard shouting behind me.

"Harry, will you hurry up? Everyone will be out of the ground in a minute and we need to get back to the car."

I could see the lads were keen to go. "Alright, alright, I am coming," I said as I waved goodbye to the Irish fans.

I got to the door of our people carrier, which was parked a few streets away from the ground.

"I have nicked your seat," Brian said as he opened the window. "You'll have to sit there."

"I suppose I'll have to then!" I laughed.

We made our way out of Latina and back to the hotel. It was going to take a couple of hours.

I soon drifted off. The next thing I remember, I am lying in a hospital bed.

Apparently we had got onto a dangerous road, quite notorious for accidents. It had two lanes, but people would always overtake. Three young boys who were in the army, they were only around 17 and 18, had been out celebrating Italy's win. They were now on the same road as us and coming towards us in their Volkswagen Golf at 90 miles per hour. They hit us head on and there was a huge, loud explosion. Our minibus catapulted into the air and landed upside down.

Their car was a wreck, smashed to pieces, and our minibus was like a scrunched-up crisp packet. Michael dragged us all out, one by one. By the time he got to me, I was covered in petrol, panicking that I was about to be blown up in the wreckage.

I was told I was lying on the road on my back, no doubt in shock. The emergency services arrived and thought I was a goner, so they put a blanket over my head. I even had my watch taken from me, God knows by who.

Once at hospital, doctors told me I had fractured my skull, broken a few bones and I had a horrible cut on my leg.

Our driver was also in the hospital. He had broken almost every bone in his body as he took the full brunt of the impact. He was in a real mess and was in hospital for about a year after the crash. Michael's son Adam was lying in the bed next to me.

It was when I finally regained consciousness that I was told about Brian. He didn't make it. And neither did the three young lads – they all died on impact.

I was devastated. I couldn't believe that Brian had gone.

'His poor wife, Hazel,' was my first thought. 'How is she going to take this news?'

Then I suddenly remembered Brian's daughter, Michelle, was expecting a baby and that he will never get to meet his grandchild.

I felt sick. He was just 47 years old and had so much life ahead of him.

Then the guilt set in. Brian was in my seat. Things could have been very different. It could have been me. If I hadn't been mucking around at the pizza place with those fans, then I could have been in that seat. I only had a few broken bones and bruises. Brian had gone. I felt very, very lucky to be alive.

Back home, Jim Nolan, the Bournemouth chairman, had called Sandra to tell her about the crash. She had been worried sick after not hearing from me.

When I eventually spoke to her I could tell she was frantic, so I got Jamie on the phone.

"Whatever you do, don't bring your mum here," I told him. I just thought it would be too much for her.

So Mark and Jamie made their way from Heathrow to Rome to come and see me, while Sandra stayed at home. To be honest, I didn't want the boys seeing me in that state either, but I was glad Sandra was staying at home. I would have been worried about her if she came too.

I remember them approaching my bed in hospital, really slowly, almost scared. I think they were worried about what they were going to see. I was still badly bruised, covered in cuts and scabs and had bandages on my face and legs. It was so great to see them.

"Dad!" they both said. And then Jamie hits the floor. He has only fainted after seeing the state I was in! He was taken into a side room by doctors and given a cold flannel. Mark goes in to check on him. "We don't need any more Redknapps unconscious," he jokes.

Jamie returned to my bedside and he just stared at me, and I am wondering how bad I look. Later, he tells me that he was so shocked as he realised I could have died that day. The boys visited me every afternoon after that, giving me updates on England's quarter-final versus Cameroon and, then our semi-final against West Germany. I would have

Where it began Four years after our first meeting in the Two Puddings, Harry and I were married in 1968 – but broke down on our way to our honeymoon in Torquay

Bridesmaids An early snap of me with my baby sister at a wedding. Pat is on the right

Growing family The first addition to our family was the mischievous boxer dog, Matty. Soon after, our first-born, Mark, came along

Along comes Jamie By 1973 Mark had a little brother – which was a bit of a shock because we'd convinced ourselves Jamie was going to be a girl! With two boys in the house, none of Sarn's ornaments were safe!

Exciting ride Mark and Jamie weren't too keen on academic education but they were very active boys and loved spending time riding their bikes and playing football. They are pictured below with Sarn's dad's wife Renée

Class on the grass This 1970-71 West Ham team photo shows some of the quality players I was lucky enough to play with, including Bobby Moore, Frank Lampard Sr, Geoff Hurst, Jimmy Greaves, Billy Bonds and Trevor Brooking

Beach buddies Sarn and the boys on holiday

American dream We absolutely loved the lifestyle in the United States when Harry's career took us to Seattle and Phoenix – but the adventure had to be cut short

The boys Me with my dad, Harry, plus Mark and Jamie. Harry Snr loved football and was delighted when I signed for West Ham. He'd also go up to Liverpool on the train to watch Jamie play – usually with cheese and mustard pickle sandwiches to hand out!

Hospital drama
I was happy to find Harry still alive and recovering well after a car crash in Italy – but good friend Brian Tiler tragically died

Enjoying nights out
We go for dinner fairly regularly, but we're both home bodies really. Pictured left and below – with Frank Lampard Snr and Sarn's much loved and missed baby sister, Pat

Book launch
Me and Sarn with Mark and my mum and dad, Harry and Violet, at the launch of a book I did a good few years back

Chip off the old block The time Jamie spent training with Bournemouth instead of going to school paid off...luckily. I could see he had talent from a young age. It wasn't long before he was moving on to bigger and better things

Eye on the ball Life on the touchline can be stressful sometimes so it's great if you have a helpful assistant – in this case, Mark's son, Harry Jnr

Money worries The court case to clear my name over an allegation of tax evasion led to a difficult time in our lives – but Sarn never got angry with me. And it was a relief when the verdict came through

Under pressure Pictured with Sir Alex Ferguson, it looks like I'm feeling the strain here. If we have a bad result I'm still in a terrible mood when I get home – as I'm sure Sarn would agree!

loved to have been at that game, but Brian would have loved it more.

The day before the final, West Germany v Argentina, I reached over to the side of my hospital drawer and pulled out my tickets. "You've got to go," I told the boys.

"I don't want to," Jamie said.

"Go! You will have a great time," I said.

After the final, Jamie flew back alone while Mark stayed with me to help bring me home. The club arranged for me to fly back on a Euro Assist, a specially chartered medical aircraft, which set them back about £10,000. It flies at a low altitude to protect the fractures and swelling on my skull. It felt like the journey went on forever.

I was taken to Nuffield Hospital in Bournemouth and Sandra was there when I arrived. She was with me every single day until I came out.

She had been worried sick. She was relieved to see me, of course, but she felt so guilty. Brian's wife, Hazel, had the police knock on her door to tell her he had been killed – Sandra had a different phone call. Sandra and Hazel had become friends, so it hit her hard too.

It was an absolute tragedy losing Brian, and the three young boys in the other car as well. It was a terrible loss of life. It really does show you that in life, you never know what is around the corner. One minute your life is great, you are making plans to watch England play in the World Cup with your mates, then out of nowhere, in a moment, everything changes.

Did the crash make me look at life differently? Yes, I think when you have been so close to something like that, you really have to try and enjoy every day.

Chapter 13

One step at a time

'The boys would bring him the Racing Post every day, and would walk up to the local restaurant to get Harry his favourite meal, chicken Milanese and spaghetti arrabiata, even though he couldn't taste a thing'

Sandra

"I'll look after the kids for you," I told my friend Yvonne. She and her husband, Keith, lived down the road from us in Whitfield Park, and they wanted to go out for dinner.

Harry was in Italy with Brian Tiler and a couple of other football friends watching the World Cup, so with no other plans that night, I offered to watch their children. Jamie, who was at home, offered to come with me.

"Can we watch the Italy vs Ireland game?" he said as soon as we got there.

"Go on then," I smiled at him. Jamie was so excited about this tournament. We knew Harry and Brian and their friends were at the game.

I had spoken to Harry just a few hours earlier and they were excited. Harry must have called me three times a day while he was in Italy. He would fill me in on where they had been. He sounded really happy and having the time of his life.

So when he didn't call me after the Italy versus Ireland game, a really horrible feeling washed over me.

"I am worried," I said to Jamie as we arrived home.

"He will be alright, Mum," he said. "He is probably travelling back to the hotel."

"No, Jamie, I can feel it. I can feel something bad has happened," I told him.

An hour or so later, the house phone rings. My shoulders drop and my heart is relieved. "Harry?" I said, as I picked up the phone. It wasn't Harry. It was Jim.

My heart hit my stomach. "What has happened?" I asked in a panic.

"There has been an accident. Harry was involved in a crash, but he is okay," Jim said.

I feel like I have stopped breathing. "He is in hospital. But Sandra," he paused. "Brian has died."

"Oh my God!" My first thought went to Hazel, who I had become friends with through Harry and Brian. I felt heartbroken for her. Brian was a lovely man and Harry thought the world of him. I couldn't believe a trip to watch football had ended in such a tragedy.

I needed to go and see Harry in hospital. I needed to see how bad he was.

"Jamie and I are going to Italy," Mark told me. They didn't want me to go and see Harry in a bad way, and neither did Harry. But I didn't want them to see him like that, either. I had been told he had fractured his skull and had been unconscious, and I could just imagine what terrible state he would be in. But the boys were adamant they would go and bring Harry home.

It felt like forever until he arrived back in Bournemouth. I remember feeling very emotional when I first saw him. I had images in my head of what he might look like, but the reality was different. He was covered in bruises and bandages. It broke my heart to see him like that and I couldn't help but cry. He looked quite vulnerable, and I've never seen Harry like that. I just wanted to squeeze him so tightly and never let him go anywhere again. Even now, when I recall the moment I got the call and think back to that time, I feel very emotional and I find it difficult to think about.

I never left his side. Cards and flowers arrived at the hospital from family, friends and other well-wishers, and we stuck them up around Harry's bed.

He was finding it difficult to process the crash; he couldn't remember what had happened and he couldn't stop thinking about Brian.

One day, he told me that he had a flashback from the crash where he felt like he was going into a tunnel and someone was pulling him back. I knew this crash was going to have a long-term effect on Harry. We tried to bring him round and make things as normal as possible for him. The boys would bring him the *Racing Post* every day, and would walk up to the local restaurant to get Harry his favourite meal, chicken Milanese and spaghetti arrabiata, even though he couldn't taste a thing. He had lost his taste and smell as a result of the crash and it took a good six months for his taste to come back slowly, but even to this day he still can't smell a thing. Long-term, he was also left with a facial tick, though I barely notice it now as it is part of him.

I could see Harry was becoming frustrated lying in a hospital bed. "When can I get out of here?" he asked his doctor.

"We need to take one step at a time," he replied.

Harry wanted to get back to football as quickly as possible. I could tell he was feeling useless and wanted to get back to doing what he loved.

"It could take you up to six months to recover," the doctor said.

I could see Harry's expression change. There is no way he is going to sit around for six months to recover.

One step at a time

I would say it was about two months after the crash that Harry was back at work – but not on the sidelines or in the dressing room. He had a friend who would drive him to games, and Harry would sit in the crowd with a bobble hat on and coat and blend in with everyone. He was desperate to see what the players were doing, if they were playing well, if changes needed to be made. And not only that, but Jamie was now playing for Bournemouth, so for Harry it was more important than ever to get back to work.

Chapter 14

A chip off the old block

'There were times when Frank and Jamie would have to play against each other – Frank for West Ham and Jamie for Liverpool. They had come a long way from kicking balls against birdcages in the garden'

Harry

I never had any doubts that Jamie was going to make it as a footballer. Even when he was five or six I could see he had a fantastic talent.

He spent his youth playing for Tottenham, but when he left school at the age of 16, he signed for me at Bournemouth.

Leaving the Tottenham youth team wasn't that easy though; it was probably harder for me than it was for Jamie! Terry Venables was the manager and I had a lot of respect for him. Jamie had decided that he wanted to go.

"I don't want to play there, Dad," he told me one day.

"What? Why not?" I asked, totally sidelined by what he was telling me. "It is Tottenham, they are a good club."

"I don't want to play in the youth team and then make it into the first team. I don't want to be there for another three years and not play in the league," he said.

Another player who Jamie shared digs with had already told him how hard it was to break into the first team.

"But Jamie, if you knuckle down and push yourself, you will get there," I tried to reason.

"I'd rather come and play with you at Bournemouth, Dad," he said. "I will get in the first team and will be playing in a league. This is what I want."

Ultimately it was Jamie's decision and there was no changing his mind. I could tell from his face that he had really thought it all through. Still, I wasn't happy. While I admired him for speaking up and doing what he wanted to do, I was the one who had to go and tell Terry that he didn't want to stay. And worse than that, I had to tell Terry he was coming to play for me.

I called Terry and asked him if Jamie and I could come up to White Hart Lane for a chat. Jamie was dreading it, even though this was all down to him, and, to be honest, so was I.

When we walked into his office, Terry started telling us about all these players he wants to sign and his plans for Jamie.

This is going to be awkward, I thought. But it was time to rip off the plaster and tell him where Jamie stood.

Terry looked surprised. "Why does he want to leave us, Harry?" he said before turning to Jamie. "I have big plans for you, Jamie."

"He doesn't want to come to Tottenham, Terry, he won't get a game," I told him, then I braced myself.

"He is coming to play for me at Bournemouth," I said.

It went silent. He wasn't happy. In fact, in the end we had a bit of a falling out over it, but Jamie had made his mind up. We thrashed out how Jamie leaving was going to work for the club – Tottenham will take a healthy percentage of any future transfer fee – and then that was that. Jamie was a Bournemouth player.

He played just 13 games for me at Bournemouth before he attracted the attention of Liverpool manager Kenny Dalglish.

"I want to sign him," Kenny told me.

"He won't get in the team, Kenny," I said. "He doesn't want to sit on the bench, he wants to play."

"He will get into the team very quickly," Kenny assured me. Again, this was a decision for Jamie, who by this point was 17. I let Jamie duck out of training for three or four days after Kenny invited him up there for a week.

Jamie loved it. Within days, Kenny signed him for £350,000, making Jamie one of the most expensive teenage transfers in English football at that time.

Within a week, Kenny was gone when he resigned after a 4-4 draw at Everton in an FA Cup replay. I hate seeing good managers go. And Kenny was a good man and Jamie loved him.

Graeme Souness came in as manager and Jamie's career took off. At the age of 18, Jamie became the youngest Liverpool player to play in a European competition when they played Auxerre in the UEFA Cup in 1991.

Jamie got into football in a similar way to me. He would knock a ball around with his mates at any opportunity he got – including in the playground after school when he was waiting for me to pick him up. He had even got his teachers involved when they should have been marking homework!

I was the same, really. I wasn't ever without a football.

I remember when we moved to the Burdett Estate and thinking it was paradise. Not only did we have our own bathroom, but we had a big playground where you could play football – though we were not meant to and always got told off by the porters.

There were loads of us kids, just passing the ball around in our own little paradise – and that is how most of us started with football.

There was a guy who lived on the estate called Albert Chamberlain, a hard nut but a lovely man. He was also a docker and had a son called Alan, who was my mate.

Me, Alan and a few of the other boys were out one night, we were probably only about eight or nine years old, and the porters came and chased us off the grass.

"Why don't you leave them alone?" Albert said.

"They are not allowed to play on the grass," a porter snapped back. I remember thinking he was brave. You wouldn't want to argue with Albert Chamberlain, I thought.

"I tell you what, I have had enough of this," Albert said, turning his attention to us.

"I am going to start a team. We will call it the Burdett Boys and I will get you into a league and you won't have to worry about getting chased off the grass by this lot again."

I loved Albert. He had never started a team before, but he was so desperate for us to have the freedom to play that he was willing to take us on. He roped in a couple of his mates, Albert Birkett, and a man called Mr Isaac.

He ended up finding a league that we could join, the Regent's Boys' League all the way over in west London. Not only that, he had only gone and put us forward for the U12s and we were only nine! But it didn't bother us that the opposing teams towered over us, or that they were three years older. We had that east London grit and determination, and Albert made us feel as though we could take anyone on.

A chip off the old block

Every Sunday, we would all trek across London to play. We would get the bus or train everywhere and we walked for miles and miles. No one had cars.

We would all walk to Mile End station like a bunch of scruffy little urchins, all with our kit bags drowning us on our backs, our legs covered in bruises. We would then change at Aldgate, get a train, then another to Regent's Park and then we would have to walk to the place in the park where we were playing. No wonder we were fit! Then we would find a tree to get changed under – we would all strip off and get into our kits. There was no luxury of a changing room. Albert got us to sell raffle tickets to pay for our shirts and we played in all kinds of weather, rain, sun, snow, everything.

I remember one day it was so cold, we had to ask Albert to tie the laces on our boots as our hands were frozen. And I remember my mate George played in his duffle coat with his shirt over it. But we loved it. It wasn't long before we all started playing for the East London Boys, too. We would play at Hackney Marshes on a Saturday morning, then on a Sunday we would play for Burdett Boys. I loved football so much I even offered to play for the other teams. I remember being in the U12s and playing in the morning and then hanging around for a couple of hours waiting for the U13s to arrive, and then I would play for them too. Mum would pack me a cheese and mustard pickle sandwich for me to have in between.

Eventually we all went on to get apprenticeships. It turned out that every boy on that team signed for a club. Roger Hoy played for Tottenham with Peter Peck, Georgie Jacks went off to Millwall, Johnny Blake went to QPR, Peter Jenkins went to Chelsea and Colin Mackleworth was with me at West Ham. Our mate Terry Reardon went to Tottenham and played in the reserves with Jimmy Greaves, but he never made it and I will never know why. He was the best footballer at school, a big lad, but good. These days he is a taxi driver and we have stayed in touch.

My friend Alan, Albert's son, was tragically killed in a car accident on the Breckland bypass, when he was 20. Obviously Albert was devastated; we all were. But I made sure I looked after Albert, it is what Alan would have wanted. When I went to West Ham, Albert would come along and watch us train. And when I became manager years later, Albert would come and watch the team train. He would get the bus to Chadwell Heath every day and loved it. Sometimes he would bring his mates, and they would all stand watching the boys play, and I would make sure they all got a cup of tea. West Ham was their team and the club belonged to them, that was my view. That was why I always loved having them there. And it was the least I could do after what Albert did for us as kids. In some ways, it was my way of paying him back. Albert not only had faith in us and brought us together as a team, but he taught us determination and that you can achieve anything if you put your mind to it. I instilled that same mantra in both Mark and Jamie. Jamie has always known what he wanted, and even though it was an awkward conversation to have with Terry when he left Spurs, Jamie made the right call.

But while Jamie's career was taking off at Liverpool, my managerial career at Bournemouth was slowly coming to an end. Things hadn't been the same since Brian had died. I was feeling low, I missed my mate terribly, but also the club was changing. Ken Gardiner was now the chairman and we had a falling out – one I felt we didn't ever come back from.

It was the last home game of the season and we had just beaten Reading 3-2. We were looking to finish eighth and it was a good win for The Cherries fans. After the game, in the vice-president's lounge, Ken was about to make a speech about a barman who had worked at the club for almost two decades. Just as Ken was about to talk to the staff and players, our centre-half Kevin Bond walked in, and not realised there was about to be a speech, he ordered a drink. Ken wasn't happy and had a pop at him in front of all of us – and that didn't make me happy. You don't have a go at people in front of others.

After the speech, I pulled him to one side and had a word – but things quickly escalated when he said something very hurtful about Brian. I saw red. I wasn't having that. I grabbed him by the throat and a scuffle broke out. We were pulled apart. We had one more game to go and I knew that would be my last.

At the end of the 1991-92 season, I quit. Billy Bonds, who was managing my old club, West Ham, had called me after they were relegated, and wanted me to join him as his assistant.

Don't get me wrong, I had an absolutely fantastic time at Bournemouth during that period, but with Brian no longer there, it just didn't feel right and it was time to move on.

I had been at West Ham for a year when my nephew, Frank, signed for the youth team. Like Jamie, he had shown a lot of promise and talent at a young age, and was on the club's books by the time he was 16.

Three years later, I became the manager when Billy Bonds resigned and Frank Sr became my assistant. Frank Jr had been sent out on loan to Swansea City, and after a brief spell there, in 1996 he came back to play for the first team under me.

Being a football manager isn't an easy job – especially when it involves your family. With every decision you make, there will always be someone who doesn't like it – be it the player, the fans or the board. Sometimes even the player's wife! When you are in the world of football, it has an effect on the whole family. And I know that more than most.

Managing Frank Jr was both amazing and difficult – it really wasn't easy and there were times when things became a bit complicated. I remember Frank Sr and I had words over Frank's wages.

"He needs more money," Frank Sr told me one day.

"Frank, that is not down to me mate, you know that," I told him.

"It is just not good enough Harry, I'm sorry, he needs to be earning more than he is," he replied.

It went back and forth for a while, it all became a bit tense, then I told him to take it to the chairman. He wasn't happy.

Frank Jr was also getting a lot of stick from the fans for playing for the club where his uncle was the boss and his dad was the assistant, so some people thought he didn't deserve it. It broke my heart at some of the abuse he had to suffer in the stands, from home fans and away. I don't remember Jamie ever getting the same level of abuse when he played under me at Bournemouth. People just seemed to have it in for Frank. Anyone else would have wilted under that level of negativity and pressure, but not Frank Jr.

Then there were the jibes about his weight. The fans could be really cruel, but Frank Jr never let it faze him. He was very disciplined and always trained hard. If I told the lads to do 10 laps, he would do 20. If I called an end to training, he would stay another hour. His dad was the same when he was a player, except Frank Jr probably had more of a natural talent for the game. He just had to work harder to prove it to people.

He was very determined, and he did go on to prove everyone wrong. He went on to become one of the great players in the game. He is such a strong character, even now as a manager, and has always been focused.

Of course, there were the times when Frank and Jamie would have to play against each other – Frank for West Ham and Jamie for Liverpool. They had come a long way from kicking balls against birdcages in the garden, and they had both inherited their mums' competitive streaks.

I remember going up to Anfield one season and Jamie caught Frank with quite a nasty tackle. Frank had to come off for treatment.

My goalkeeping coach at the time was Les Sealey, a fantastic man who we lost far too early after he died of a heart attack at the age of 43 in 2001.

Les pulled Frank to one side. "Oi, you get back on that pitch and you do him," Les told him. "You go back on there, and make sure you do Jamie good and proper."

I was sitting there overhearing this thinking, 'Hang on a minute, Les is telling Frank to go and take my son out.'

I couldn't say to Les, "Leave it out, that is my son." So I didn't say anything. Luckily, Frank went back on the pitch, took the tackle for what it was and behaved himself. Jamie was in the clear. Frank didn't get his revenge on Jamie until he moved to Chelsea. And he got his revenge alright. He caught

A chip off the old block

Jamie with his elbow and smashed his lips – Jamie had to have 30 stitches in his face.

Both Frank and Jamie have always been competitive, but that is what made them great footballers. And off the pitch they were very close; they still are to this day. In fact, Jamie was by Frank's side when he made his England debut against Belgium at the Stadium of Light in 1999. That was a proud moment for the whole family. And at least while on the same team, we could sit and enjoy the game knowing they weren't going to tear strips out of each other.

Chapter 15

A day we'll never forget

*'I am on my way to the hospital now, Sarn,'
he told me. 'She is absolutely beautiful,
Harry,' I told him. 'Just wait till you see her.'*

Sandra

"I have met a girl, Mum." I must say I wasn't that surprised.
Mark was absolutely gorgeous – both my boys were, they are!
– and Mark had all the girls after him. I know all mums say
that about their sons, we are biased of course, but Mark really
was handsome. After his football career was cut horribly short,
he was signed up by a modelling agency.

"Her name is Rachel," he said. Harry and I were delighted.
Mark was in his early 20s and we were happy that he had
met a nice girl. We liked Rachel a lot and got on well with

her. She had a two-year-old boy called Luke from a previous relationship and Mark doted on him. He loved kids and was brilliant with them.

Rachel was from Bournemouth and had lived there her whole life. And perhaps, in hindsight, that might have been where some of their problems came from further down the line. Mark had been born and bred in London, and I suppose things were different growing up compared to the quiet parts of Bournemouth. There is a different pace to life. Mark and Rachel were together on and off for about 10 years before splitting up. Looking back, they were probably too young to get together – it was different to how things were when Harry and I met at 17. I suppose Mark and Rachel had a bit of a love-hate relationship. They couldn't be with each other and they couldn't be without each other. Although the relationship didn't work out, we are forever grateful to Rachel for giving us our first grandchild.

In early 1999, Rachel fell pregnant and when Mark came home to tell us, we were over the moon.

Molly Violet – named after Harry's mum – was born at Poole Hospital on December 17, 1999.

But we will never forget the day Molly was born – and not just because she was our first grandchild!

Harry had been up at Birmingham the night before when West Ham played Aston Villa in the Worthington Cup quarter-final and won. He was on top of the world – his team had made the semi-finals and he had a new baby grand-daughter, which was particularly special after two sons.

"I am on my way to the hospital now, Sarn," he told me.

"She is absolutely beautiful, Harry," I told him. "Just wait till you see her."

But Harry took longer than expected. Unbeknown to us at the time, Harry took another phone call – this time from Peter Taylor, the manager at Gillingham.

"Harry, I am phoning about Emmanuel Omoyinmi," Peter told him.

"Oh, do you want him on loan again, Pete?" he replied. Emmanuel, who they all called Manny, had just signed for West Ham from Gillingham.

"No, no, it is not that," Peter said. "He played for us in the cup." He stopped for a moment, then added, "The League Cup."

Harry said he just fell silent as his heart began to sink. "He played for us in the cup, Harry, and I see you brought him on in extra time with a minute to go."

"Don't tell me that," Harry told him, realising Manny was actually cup-tied, which meant it was against the rules to play for a second team in the same competition in the same season.

He must have been in the car for a good hour, just totally lost in his thoughts, feeling all kinds of emotions. Over the years I have seen Harry low, sad, frustrated, anxious, angry – and I think after that phone call he felt all of them. He just couldn't pull himself together.

"He didn't even touch the ball, Sarn," Harry told me, when explaining why he had arrived at the hospital so late. He was pacing the room, shaking his head. "We only put him on to run down the clock."

That was it, Harry's mind was elsewhere. To say he won't ever forget the day Molly was born is an understatement.

Aston Villa had lodged a complaint and the FA were investigating. "Surely we will get a fine," Harry said to me one evening. "They can't make us replay it. I fancy our chances in the semis against Leicester."

Harry just couldn't shake it. We were days away from Christmas and all he could think about was the cup. "The fans will go potty if we have to replay, Sarn. The players aren't going to be too happy either."

Then the news came – West Ham and Aston Villa needed to replay the match. Harry did his best to enjoy Christmas, after all, we had been given the best gift of all, and it was Molly's first Christmas. But I could tell he was struggling. There had been a huge backlash over his decision to bring Manny on and Harry was bearing the brunt of it.

On January 11, West Ham replayed their match. I remember watching the game on TV with a knot in my stomach. After 47 minutes, Frankie scored – but then just ten minutes before the end, Aston Villa scored and it was going to extra time.

'Harry's heart must be pounding,' I thought to myself. I just wanted to tell him it would be okay. Except it wasn't, as Aston Villa scored two goals and were through to the semi-finals. Harry was heartbroken and I could see it in his face when he appeared in a post–match interview.

"This night will haunt me for the rest of my life," he said with sadness in his eyes. "All the right questions were asked at the time, and we were given the wrong answers.

"It is not like losing a normal match. We had already won the game once and reached the semi-finals. It is a bitter pill to swallow.

"We've got to pick ourselves up, but I don't know how I am going to put a team out on Saturday."

This was going to take Harry a long time to get over.

Chapter 16

Under pressure

'It was my 50th birthday and I couldn't celebrate. I just wanted to go home. Being a manager is a lonely job, it can be very, very isolating'

Harry

I was lying on our settee in our house in Hornchurch, looking up at the ceiling.

"I can't face going out tonight, Sarn," I said.

We had lost that day and I couldn't pull myself together. The year had got off to a terrible start after our cup replay against Aston Villa.

"Come on Harry, we can go and have a quiet dinner, it will make you feel better and take your mind off things," she said.

"Honestly Sarn, can we just stay in tonight?" I replied.

When Harry Met Sandra

Sandra has always been an amazing support throughout my whole career. To be honest, I can't tell you the amount of times she has brought me back up after a disastrous result. Jamie always says I won the lottery when I married Sandra, and he is 100 per cent right. She knows what to say when I am in a low mood – and she has seen me in some terrible, low, low moods over the years – and she doesn't ever push me.

When I am feeling like that, Sandra is the only person I can talk to.

I remember that day when I was lying on the sofa, it was a bad day, really tough. We were struggling at West Ham and had a poor run of results. Looking up at that ceiling, I felt like I was close to almost cracking up.

It wasn't the first time I had felt like this. It happened several times over my career. There was one match that I won't ever forget because it was the day before my 50th birthday. The whole family had travelled up to Birmingham for the weekend. Jamie's Liverpool were taking on Aston Villa at Villa Park, but the day before West Ham were playing Leeds a couple of hours away. Sandra had booked a nice Italian restaurant for all of us to celebrate, and had bought me this lovely watch. All the family had gathered at the restaurant, waiting for me to return.

But instead of riding on the crest of a wave after a win, we lost 1-0 and were hovering at the bottom of the table. We had lost to Derby, Blackburn and Arsenal. Leeds had already beaten us at home in January. I just couldn't snap out of it. I was like a zombie. I couldn't speak to anyone. It was my 50th birthday and I couldn't celebrate. I just wanted to go home.

Being a manager is a lonely job, it can be very, very isolating. You just feel you're under so much pressure all the time. You've got no friends – you go from being one of the lads in the changing room, laughing and joking with all the other footballers to then being on your own.

I have known players who went on to become coaches or managers, and they just found it too much. I know people who went into management and found the pressure unbearable. I have seen people, friends, have breakdowns. People get carried away with managers. You get one bad result and that is it, the fans and the press are on you. But a manager needs good players.

It is very different being a coach, you can take a bit of training in the morning, a bit of banter with the players, and they like you. Then the manager comes in, picks the team, someone doesn't like it and you've got the players hating you; his mates, his wife – even the kids hate you.

Then you get grief from the fans. I remember a few losses where I have driven home and seen people in the car next to me just staring. 'What are they thinking? Do they blame me? Is this my fault? Do they want me sacked?!' It was just awful.

Some people might say that managers get rewarded and paid a decent wage, and yes, of course they do, especially these days, but for me, it is not about the money. It never has been. It is about how you feel as a person. You want to be successful. You know your pride is at stake. You don't want to be a failure.

Sandra and I would never make arrangements to go out on a Saturday night after a game, in case whoever I was managing at the time got beat and I couldn't pull myself out of it. I couldn't talk to anybody. I would eat my pasta or a pizza and have a glass of wine, but I would do it all in silence. I couldn't go out with anyone else. But I always feel comfortable with Sandra. She would always say I was never good company after a bad game. And she is right. I used to get very, very low.

I always used to worry about what I would do if I didn't succeed. I was thinking about what am I going to do with my life. I didn't know anything. I had never done anything else. I couldn't be an electrician or a carpenter, I would be useless. I couldn't write. It really was very difficult at times. But Sandra always made me feel better – and she has done that throughout our marriage.

Chapter 17

A wedding in Bermuda

'Jamie and Louise got married around the same time David Beckham was dating Victoria Adams, so there was a lot of interest in footballers' wives and girlfriends – the WAGs as they were called. You didn't have that in mine and Tina Moore's day, thankfully!'

Sandra

"Mum, it's Jamie, we've got something to tell you." He paused, but I could hear the excitement in his voice and giggling in the background. "Louise and I are getting married!"

Harry and I were in France where we had been watching the 1998 World Cup when Jamie called with the news.

"We are getting married in Bermuda... this week," he said.

"Bermuda! Married! Harry, we've got to get a flight home!" I said.

Jamie and Louise had met through their mutual friend, Robbie Williams. Jamie and Robbie had been close friends for years, and when Robbie quit Take That in 1995, he moved in with Jamie at his digs. They knew the newspapers wouldn't find him there.

Eternal, the band Louise was in, were supporting Take That when Robbie introduced them backstage. I think they went out a few times, before deciding to be friends. Louise would later say that Jamie being a footballer held her back from starting a relationship – I suppose they could all be a bit wild back then! – but eventually they were in a relationship and things were serious. Really serious – our youngest son was about to get married.

Harry and I rushed home from France and picked up our outfits – I chose a beige palm print dress – then we were straight on a plane to Bermuda.

News of the wedding had got out and Hello! and OK! were in a bidding war for the exclusive pictures. Hello! had offered a crazy six figure fortune but Jamie and Louise were quite a private couple and turned it down.

"You are mad!" Harry told him when we met them at the hotel. "Why haven't you taken the money?"

But Jamie and Louise were adamant. They had chosen to get married in Bermuda away from the limelight back home and they wanted to keep it low key.

Three days after Jamie popped the question, he married Louise in a beautiful ceremony on board an 80-foot white yacht called Lady Erica on June 29 – the day before mine and Harry's 31st wedding anniversary.

Louise looked absolutely stunning in a white chiffon dress and I remember how relaxed she looked when she arrived with her mum, Lynne, on a horse-drawn carriage. She had a blue butterfly clip in her hair and I remember they matched the butterflies on her strappy shoes.

There were only about 30 of us at the wedding. Mark was his best man, and Jamie's Liverpool team-mate Phil Babb had also flown out to be there. My parents were no longer around, but I know Harry was sad that his own parents couldn't make it, as they didn't want to fly. They had a lovely reception at the Marriott Castle Harbour Hotel, which overlooked the harbour. It really was a beautiful evening.

The next day, grainy pictures of the wedding appeared in the newspapers. "They got what they wanted anyway," Harry said. "You should have taken the money!" Even now, Harry is still stunned that they turned down a small fortune for those pictures.

After the wedding, the press attention on them both grew. Louise's solo career was taking off after she had decided to quit Eternal two years earlier, and she was on the cover of all the magazines. Meanwhile, Jamie had been nicknamed a 'Spice

Boy' by the tabloids – we always used to laugh at that, although never really sure what it meant – and he was getting papped for the first time off the pitch.

Jamie and Louise got married around the same time David Beckham was dating Victoria Adams, so there was a lot of interest in footballers' wives and girlfriends – the WAGs as they were called. You didn't have that in mine and Tina Moore's day, thankfully!

But Jamie and Louise were never a showbizzy couple. They were always both very down to earth.

Jamie spent his childhood around the likes of Bobby Moore and Geoff Hurst, but we always kept him grounded, both boys grounded. Harry was always set on that. You don't forget where you came from.

When Jamie was at Liverpool, his grandad, Harry's dad, would go up on the train and watch him play every Saturday. He would always take him a cheese and mustard pickle sandwich made by his nan. At this point in Jamie's career, he had dieticians at the club and could afford to eat in the best restaurants if he wanted, but he loved that cheese and mustard pickle sandwich that his nan made him every week.

I remember there was one day when Jamie and his team-mate Steve McManaman, he was a lovely boy, had driven Harry's dad to the train station.

"I feel terrible," Harry's dad told him when he got back. "I took a cheese sandwich for Jamie, but I didn't take one for his friend Steve.

"Pop, Macca is on about £60,000 a week, he doesn't need a cheese and pickle roll," Harry told him.

"No, I'm not having that," he said. "I am going to get your mum to make me an extra one for him."

Harry's dad started taking two lots of cheese and mustard pickle sandwiches up with him on the train. And Steve loved them as much as Jamie. I think footballers can get a bit carried away sometimes, especially with the money they earn these days, and I love how Jamie had kept his feet on the ground – all while eating his nan's sandwiches!

And, despite being a huge pop star at the time, Louise was a very normal girl, too.

Harry and I would rather have a night in than a night out. And Louise and Jamie were very much the same.

In July 2004, Jamie and Louise welcomed their first son Charley and Beau followed four years later.

Sadly, they divorced in 2018 but sometimes that's just what happens. All you can wish for is that your children are happy and we will be forever grateful to them both for our beautiful grandsons.

Chapter 18

Taking sides

'I don't care what people say about me, I've heard all sorts in the stands during my career, but to bring Sandra into it was disgusting and I was furious'

Harry

"Mark has a new girlfriend. I met her earlier today." I was on my way home from a game and was calling Sandra to tell her where I was. "Her name is Lucy, and she seems really nice," Sandra said.

Mark first met his now wife Lucy about 20 years ago at an event when Jamie was playing for Tottenham. At the time, Lucy was expecting a baby with a famous boy band singer and Mark was coming to the end of his relationship with Rachel. Lucy's relationship with the singer eventually broke down and Mark and Rachel couldn't work things out, so about a year or so later they got together.

Sandra went on to tell me how, when she got home, Mark and Lucy were in the kitchen with the little baby, a girl called Emilie, in a baby carrier and her big brother Joe running around. "They are adorable!" she said.

Mark was on top of the world. He absolutely doted on his daughter Molly and now he had two more children to look after. Anyone who knows Mark will tell you how soft he is and how much he loves babies and children. Sandra always says he would have had nine if he could! If there is a baby, Mark is there with them, he is like the pied piper. But I suppose I am like that, really. Being an only child, I love that we have a big family with lots of grandchildren. I love to hear them laugh and play. I hate it when you have houses that are like show homes and the kids can't have fun in them. Houses are to be lived in. I remember when we got our new cream sofas and two of the grandkids drew on them with a biro. Sandra went mad.

"They are kids, Sarn," I told her. "It will come out!" Our two used to smash our house to pieces with footballs when they were younger! There was always broken glass or a wonky picture frame somewhere.

Mark eventually proposed to Lucy, and they got married at the Chewton Glen Hotel in Hampshire in 2006 when Lucy was pregnant with Harry.

When Harry Met Sandra

It was a wonderful wedding. It was quite small and just family, but it was a lovely day. Molly and Emelie were flower girls. For Sandra and I to see both our boys settled down and married with children of their own was nice.

And both their families continue to grow. Jamie recently had another little boy, Raphael, who we all call Rafa, and Mark is a Pop himself as Lucy's son Joe has a little boy called Hendrix. Mark absolutely dotes on him. He dotes on all of them.

It was nice for me and Sandra to see both Mark and Jamie settle down with their wives – me and Sandra both adored Louise and Lucy – and to see them start their own families.

The late 90s felt like a good time for us, and family life was getting better and better. But while life at home was fantastic, my career was going pear-shaped.

In 2001, I left West Ham after my contract ran out. The chairman, Terry Brown, refused to renew it. My beloved West Ham, after seven years as manager of the club, I was out of a job. West Ham is a club that will always be dear to me. As a manager or a player, when you move clubs, your support moves with them, but I have always had a soft spot for the Hammers. It was my local club, it was my first club, and it was a club I loved managing. I didn't want to leave.

My downfall came when I did an interview for a West Ham fanzine. I spoke about things that the chairman wasn't very happy with. And looking back, I did say something I shouldn't have. The guy who ran the fanzine was a bloke called Gary Firmager, and he was a huge West Ham fan. Loved everything about the game and the club. I would often give him an official interview for the magazine. Long story short, he was grilling me about the money the club made off the back of the sale of Rio Ferdinand and how the £18 million was being spent. But what wasn't taken into account was how much we'd saved on Rio with wages and bonuses. I ended up saying something along the lines of, "Terry thinks he is an accountant, but he can't add up."

The interview came out around the same time I was due to talk to Terry about extending my contract. I had two years left and was confident I was going to be staying. But as soon as I walked into Terry's office, I could tell from his face that my card was marked. He told me he wasn't happy about the interview, that he didn't appreciate me saying that he couldn't add up and then he ended by saying he wouldn't be renewing my contract. And it wasn't just me losing my job; Frank Snr and my goalkeeping coach Les Sealey were going too.

"That is really not fair," I told him. "It is me you're not happy with, they haven't done anything wrong."

But Terry had made his mind up. I was absolutely gutted for Frank Sr. He was West Ham through and through and loved the club more than anyone there. And now he has lost his job – all because of me. I had to go home and break the news to Sandra. I was out of work again. But as always, she was supportive and told me it was going to be okay, even though I didn't believe her.

Looking back, I shouldn't have done that interview. I was out of order and I went a step too far with Terry. But I will tell you one thing, he never held it against me. Years later, when Rupert Lowe, the Southampton chairman, asked him for a reference, he gave me a brilliant one. And he didn't have to do that.

After West Ham, I joined Portsmouth as director of football. It was a bit of a fancy title, and to be honest I wasn't even sure what it meant when Milan Mandaric offered me the job. Ultimately, he wanted me to bring players in. One of them was Peter Crouch, but more about that transfer later.

I had only been director of football for a few months before I became manager. I was worried about managing again to be honest, it comes with so much pressure and stress. But then again, as director of football I was a glorified driver taking Milan to and from games with his mates, so the manager position became appealing.

Milan knew I needed some persuading, so he and his wife took me and Sandra for a meal at the Chewton Glen Hotel. It was a great opportunity, but I was still so reluctant to commit. I told Milan I would try it out for a year, and see if I am happy, and of course, if he is happy too. He agreed, and the next day the club announced that I was the new manager.

Taking sides

My first signing was Jim Smith. I wanted him as my assistant coach. If I am honest, I was slightly embarrassed about asking him. He had managed at Portsmouth in the 90s as well as Derby County and Oxford, so I was unsure if he'd even take it. But he did, and he was my best ever signing. We lost Jim a couple of years ago, which was devastating.

That first season in charge, with Jim by my side, we won the Championship title and were promoted to the Premier League. There's no doubt Jim played a key role in that. He knew the players, he had a great knowledge of the game and everyone loved him.

As we went up, West Ham went the other way and were relegated, but I took no pleasure in that.

Our first season in the Premier League was a tough one. We had a terrible start, but towards the end, the team knuckled down when it mattered and had some key wins that meant we were staying up. Milan was happy, or so I thought. He seemed to have an issue with Jim and I couldn't get my head around it. The fans loved Jim and would sing his name from the stands, but Milan didn't like it. He thought I should be getting all the credit. It didn't bother me. It was a team effort and I didn't care what the fans were singing as long as we were staying in the Premier League for another season. But Milan made a move to sack Jim.

I remember driving home one night and getting a call to say we were getting a new director of football, Croatian coach

Velimir Zajec. I had no idea what was going on, but I knew I wanted to work with Jim. He had more than 30 years of experience and we worked well together. My first thought was, 'What if I don't get on with Zajec?' I wasn't having it. I called Peter Storrie, the club's chief executive, and told him I was going. We prepared a joint statement and the club offered me £150,000 plus the car I had during my time there. I wasn't expecting any money, it was my decision to walk away, but Milan insisted.

I went home and spoke to Sandra and she agreed. "Give it to the local community," I told my agent. He thought I was mad, but that's what I did.

The next two weeks, I felt pretty miserable. Zajec was now the manager and I was bored at home. Sandra could see I was itching to get back into managing, and she was probably itching for me to get a job. I was no use moping around at home.

Then a call came from an agent about another job, at Portsmouth's biggest rivals, Southampton.

My first thought was that I shouldn't take it, but I'll admit I am sometimes terrible for jumping into things and not really thinking them through, and even though I discussed it with Sandra, neither of us could imagine the hate I would get when I was eventually announced as the new manager.

I remember driving to the training ground and seeing banners with 'Judas Scum' written on them. I had the same painted on the wall of my house. And then came the threats. Someone had got hold of my number and was leaving voicemail after voicemail. "I hope you get cancer," was one, "I hope your wife gets cancer," came another. "I hope you crash your car and kill your wife." I was angry.

I don't care what people say about me – I've heard all sorts in the stands during my career – but to bring Sandra into it was disgusting and I was furious. At the time, we lived by the beach and she would hear people calling me scum, and this and that, not nice stuff that a lady should be hearing, let alone about her husband. She was understandably upset, and that was a step too far for me. "What have you done, Harry?" she would say. I quickly realised the mistake I had made. And it wasn't just the Portsmouth fans who were giving me grief, Southampton had also fallen out of the Premiership for the first time in 27 years and that fell to me.

After two years in charge, I returned to Portsmouth. Alain Perrin had been sacked by Milan and there were rumours Neil Warnock was going to take charge. That was until Milan saw Frank at a Chelsea match.

"You should get Harry back in charge," Frank told him. Milan said no, telling him we had fallen out. "He would like to, you know," Frank persisted. At the time, Portsmouth were facing relegation and Frank thought I'd be the man to pull them out of it.

"Could you persuade him?" Milan asked. "I don't think I'd need to," Frank said.

And the rest is history. Within three years, Portsmouth had won the FA Cup for the first time in 69 years after beating Cardiff City in the final. It was probably one of the best achievements in my career.

Chapter 19

Losing my baby sister

'Pat passed away with her family by her side. She was 58. I felt numb. We were all utterly devastated. How could she be gone?'

Sandra

It was April 14, 2008 and Harry and I were in Spain when I got a phone call from my niece, Natalie, about my sister, Pat. It is a day I will never forget.

"It's my mum, she is in hospital," she said. My heart sank. So many horrible thoughts started running through my mind. Has she had a heart attack? Has she got a brain aneurysm just like our mum? Has she got cancer?

"They think she has pneumonia," she said.

I remember letting out a sigh of relief. 'Thank God' I thought to myself. 'It isn't anything too serious.'

But I was still very worried. My sister was in hospital and I was in another country. I remember pacing up and down the beach in a panic, and I couldn't stop myself.

"We need to go back home, Harry," I told him.

Harry and I decided to fly home straight away to visit Pat in hospital. We were so, so close and I had to be by her side.

I was also worried about Natalie, Claire and Frankie – he is just Frank in the world of football, but he has always been Frankie to us. I just kept thinking how horrible it must be for them to see their mum in hospital. They idolised her. I did too.

Over the years newspapers and magazines have referred to Pat as my twin, but she wasn't, she was my baby sister. Everyone said we looked like twins, and I can see that, especially as we got older.

It is funny as when we were younger I had blonde hair and Pat's was red, and then we switched as we got older with Pat dyeing hers blonde and me a flame-coloured red.

I guess we were as good as twins. We knew each other inside out and would tell each other everything. We would be on the phone for hours – sometimes once or twice a day.

Years ago you could have a favourite number on your land-line and calls to that number would be cheaper – mine was Pat's. Though I don't recall our phone bills being that cheap!

We would chat about the kids, what they were up to, how they were getting on at school, and as they got older, work and football. Harry and Frank would also be the topic of conversation, often whether they were driving us mad! We really would share everything.

That night, hours after the phone call, Harry and I flew into London and headed straight to Whipps Cross Hospital.

In the days earlier, Pat had been feeling a bit unwell, like she had the flu. She had a cough too.

Back in the day, if footballers were under the weather, they were told to go for a run wearing a black sack under their clothes to help sweat the flu or cold out. She was as fit as a fiddle and would often go for a run to keep fit. So that is what Pat did, but instead of making her feel better, she very quickly felt worse and was taken to hospital. Frankie pulled out of games against Wigan and Everton to be at his mum's bedside with Frank Snr and his sisters. After a couple of days, she started to show some signs of improvement, and we encouraged Frankie to go back to training ahead of Chelsea's Champions League match. That is what his mum would have wanted.

I don't think Pat ever missed one of Frank's games. She was so proud of what he had achieved and was always in the stands to support him. She loved watching him play, and he loved her watching him.

After 10 days in hospital, Pat started to deteriorate quite quickly and became gravely ill. Doctors told us she had developed meningococcal meningitis. My heart broke. I knew I was going to lose my baby sister. On Thursday April 24, Pat passed away with her family by her side. She was 58.

I felt numb. We were all utterly devastated. How could she be gone? She just had pneumonia. I had no idea it could be such a cruel killer.

My life was never going to be the same again. Natalie, Claire and Frankie's lives were never going to be the same again. Pat's grandchildren's lives would never be the same again.

Following her death, Chelsea put out a statement, which read, 'Pat was a very familiar face to many people at Chelsea. Her unswerving support for her son's career was evident at virtually every game that Frank participated in regardless of where it was being played, she would always be there to watch him with Frank's dad. Pat will be deeply missed by everyone at Chelsea.'

Suddenly everything started to become very real. We needed to start planning her funeral.

Pat and I had talked about death. It was something we were both honest and open about after losing our mum at such a young age.

"I don't want to be buried," she told me one day. "I don't want people visiting my grave like we have to with mum."

I felt the same. The thought of my family having to come and lay flowers on a grave was too much to bear. "I agree," I told her.

We held Pat's funeral at St Margaret's Church in Barking – the church where she had married Frank Snr 40 years earlier, and where I had married Harry.

It was a highly emotional day. West Ham fans lined the streets to pay their respects and some let off pink and white balloons. It was absolutely heartbreaking to see young Frankie carry his mother's coffin into the church. The children were in pieces. Some of Frankie's Chelsea friends, including John Terry, Ashley Cole, Tal Ben Haim and Shaun Wright-Phillips came to offer their condolences. They all thought so highly of Pat and wanted to support Frankie too.

Harry, Mark and Jamie were by my side throughout. It was probably the hardest day of my life.

Fourteen years on and I am still incredibly close to Pat's children. Natalie is just like Mark – they both have such kind souls. They are also a bit rebellious and I think that comes with both being the eldest. They always joke to their children about the stories they could tell about growing up together! Claire was the middle child and would always follow her older sister and big cousin around. Jamie and Frankie were close – Jamie is closer in age to Claire, but Frankie looked up to Jamie growing up and I remember many summers in Bournemouth where Pat and the kids would visit and Jamie and Frankie would be out playing football, smashing the ball against my birdcage.

Frankie's life then started to fall apart a bit after his mum died, which is only natural. He was absolutely heartbroken and doted on his mum. He was definitely a mummy's boy. His relationship with fiancée Elen Rivas, mum to his two daughters, Luna and Isla, very sadly started to break down and they eventually split up.

So when Frankie called me out of the blue one day in the autumn of 2009 to tell me he had met someone new, I could hear the happiness in his voice.

Frankie had been introduced to TV presenter Christine Bleakley by Piers Morgan at the Pride of Britain Awards – I could tell he was smitten. The newspapers would later say that he sought my approval of Christine, but he didn't and I would never want Christine to think that either. He just wanted to share his news with me and I couldn't have been happier for them both.

I remember meeting Christine for the first time. She was a beautiful girl, very tall with dark glossy hair. They seemed very much in love and I knew Pat would be happy.

Christine quickly fitted in with our family, going on beach holidays with Frankie, Jamie and Louise, and by the summer of 2011, Frankie and Christine were engaged.

They eventually got married in a beautiful ceremony at St Paul's Church in Knightsbridge in December 2015. Christine looked stunning in her white dress and you couldn't wipe the smile from Frank's face. All their family and friends were there including Holly Willoughby, Ant McPartlin, Declan Donnelly and Phillip Schofield. I couldn't believe how many celebrities there were in one room. But there was one I was most taken by.

Popping to the loos at the reception at The Arts Club, with my daughter-in-law Lucy, we were stopped by a young man with the same colour hair as me.

"I have just seen you on the TV," he said to me.

Puzzled, I replied, "But I have been here all day!"

"No," he laughed. "You were on Mr and Mrs with Harry."

It was Ed Sheeran. The biggest singer of the moment and he is telling me he has seen me on TV.

"Would you mind if we got a picture?" Lucy asked him as I started to cringe inside.

"Of course not! I would love to have a picture with Mrs Redknapp!" he smiled.

I was so embarrassed. He put his arm around me and we both smiled for the camera. The grandkids joke that he looks like part of the family, and they loved the picture so much that they had it framed for me that Christmas.

Back at the reception it was time for speeches and Frankie stood up and gave the most wonderful speech about his new wife. He spoke about how he missed his mum and how he wished she had met Christine. My eyes started to fill with tears. Looking at Christine, he told her how he could imagine them shopping together and going for afternoon tea. It is true, I could too. Pat wasn't there to see her youngest child get married, but she was definitely there in spirit. And her spirit now lives on through his daughter, who Frank and Christine chose to name after Patricia.

I remember Frankie calling me when she was born in 2008 to tell me her name. "I love it," I said, quite choked up. And I knew Pat would love it too.

Chapter 20

Matters of the heart

'Sandra was obviously worried sick. I used to worry about what the stress of the game did to me, but Sandra worried more. Even now she has to remind me to take my heart tablets as I am useless'

Harry

I never imagined when I was an 11-year-old boy playing for Tottenham that I would one day be manager. I looked up to the likes of Bill Nicholson and Danny Blanchflower and wanted to play like them. Fifty years later, I was offered the job after Juande Ramos was sacked.

As much as I loved the club – starting my own football career there, and then seeing Jamie play for them – I wasn't sure I wanted the job at first. Don't get me wrong, it was a fantastic opportunity to manage a huge club like Spurs, but

Portsmouth were going places. We were playing in the UEFA Cup and Tottenham were at the bottom of the league. My main concern though was Sandra. Managing Portsmouth, then Southampton, and back to Portsmouth again meant I was only 20 or 30 miles down the road from home. Signing as the Spurs manager came with a much bigger commitment; I'd be driving to London most of the week for training and the home games would actually be far from my home.

"I'm not sure," I told her. "I will be up and down the motorway a lot."

"You should hear them out, Harry," she said. "But whatever your decision, I will support you."

That's one of the things I love most about Sandra. Not only is she great at pulling me up when I am feeling low, but she is my biggest cheerleader and supporter. She is more level-headed than me and takes time to think things through.

She wasn't the only one who thought I should speak to Daniel Levy; Peter Storrie thought I should too.

I took the job and saved them from relegation. Spurs were on the up again, and while things in my career were looking good, my health wasn't.

During my time at Spurs, I had a procedure on my heart. I had been playing golf with Jamie one morning and we had only started the first hole when suddenly I felt like I couldn't catch my breath.

"Jamie, there is something wrong," I told him.

"What is it? What is the matter?" he said. I could tell he was worried, but he was so calm.

"I don't know," I said. I was also starting to worry, too. "I can't breathe."

"Come on," he said. He took my clubs and we got back to the clubhouse where Jamie got straight on the phone to the club.

They told him they wanted me to go straight to Whipps Cross Hospital in London to see heart specialist John Hogan. He is one of the best cardiologists in the country and was there the day former Bolton player Fabrice Muamba collapsed on the pitch at Spurs. There is no doubt the quick thinking and experience of the medical team that day saved his life.

"You have blocked arteries," Mr Hogan told me. "We will treat them with stents."

It wasn't long before I was having keyhole surgery to have them fitted. It is amazing. I was worried they would have to open me up, but Mr Hogan assured me it was a simple procedure and straightforward.

Sandra was obviously worried sick. I used to worry about what the stress of the game did to my health, but Sandra worried more. Even now she has to remind me to take my heart tablets as I am useless.

When Harry Met Sandra

I do believe that things happen for a reason and it is lucky they got me in when they did. I wouldn't have liked to take a chance on what would have happened had I not had the stents fitted.

Chapter 21

Raided

'You need to come back. The police are here. They have a warrant and are turning our house upside down. They say they are investigating corruption'

Sandra

Harry's career has had many ups and downs, but I would say even the low points have made us stronger as a couple. There have been so many tests for us along the way, but the biggest test of all was his 2012 trial for alleged tax evasion. The trial itself lasted two weeks before Harry was cleared of all charges, but the whole nightmare lasted five years. It all began at the end of November in 2007. Harry had been in Germany and I was at our home in Bournemouth alone. I had been nervous about being at home alone as our neighbour had been held at gunpoint by burglars a few nights before, but I told myself I am safe and secure in the house and have the dog.

It was a Wednesday morning, about 5.30, when our front gate buzzer went off.

I jumped out of bed, wondering who it could be at that time in the morning. As I made my way down the stairs, I wondered if it was kids mucking around – we often had people buzzing the gate and running off, but not at this time in the morning. As I went to disarm the buzzer, I saw bright lights shining through the gate. There were two cars parked outside the gate with their headlights shining directly into the house.

I was terrified. Who was it? The armed burglars came back into my mind.

I answered the buzzer.

"Hello, who is it?" I asked, shaking with fear.

"It is the police," came the reply.

The police? I suddenly felt sick. I felt like my heart had hit my stomach and I had a sinking feeling. Something must have happened to Harry. Has there been a plane crash? Is Harry okay? Has something awful happened to him? Is that why the police are here, to give me bad news?

"We've come to search the house," the police officer said.

"What for?" I asked, feeling confused.

"Mrs Redknapp, you need to open the gate and let us in," came the reply.

Raided

"You can't come in," I told them. "My husband isn't here."

"Well, we have a warrant," came the response. "We are investigating alleged corruption."

What? Corruption? Corruption of what? 'Well, they won't find anything here,' I thought. I let go of the buzzer and opened the gate. Suddenly I could see camera flashes going off, flashbulbs lighting up the driveway, men with cameras following the police to the house. What the hell is going on? 'We've been set up here,' I thought.

Within a matter of minutes, I had all these police officers in my house, they were each going through all our stuff, opening drawers and cupboards, rifling through paperwork. They were pulling stuff out of my dresser, looking at it, then throwing it back in. The house was a total mess – we looked like we had been burgled.

"When you realise that whatever you are supposedly looking for isn't here, then I would like an apology," I said to a group of officers gathered in the hall.

One stepped forward. "Mrs Redknapp, would you mind directing your questions at me please?"

From his curt manner, I sensed he was the boss.

"Well, I have a room full of people, no one has introduced themselves or told me what is going on. How am I meant to know who I should be talking to?"

The feeling of terror and fear had already passed over me, and now I was absolutely furious.

It was 7am before I called anyone to tell them what was going on. I didn't want to wake up the boys and worry them, and I didn't want Harry to panic as he was still in Stuttgart.

I scrolled through my phone, my hands shaking. I found Harry's number and hit the call button.

"Hi Sarn, are you alright?" he asked.

"No, I am bloody not alright!" I shouted back, and then I turned the air blue.

"You need to come back. The police are here," I said. "They have a warrant and are turning our house upside down. They say they are investigating corruption."

"Call Mark, stay where you are, I am coming home," he said.

Mark was at our house within minutes. He told the photographers where to go and tried to get some sense out of the police. I had the TV on and to my horror the whole thing was playing out on GMTV. What on earth has gone on for our house to be raided at dawn? Why is this on breakfast news? I have only ever wanted a quiet life, I thought.

I went into the kitchen, where a group of police officers were ransacking the cupboards.

I leant against the aga. "Do you want a cup of tea?" I asked them.

It felt like forever until they started to wind down their search. After all that fuss and the mess they made, they walked out with a computer that Harry had bought me as a

Christmas present a couple of years earlier. I don't think we had even turned it on. I didn't know how to work it and Harry definitely wouldn't have known. I think it had been taken out of the box and then put to one side. There wouldn't be any material on it, full stop, let alone what they think might be incriminating.

A few hours later, Harry was back in the UK and drove straight to Chichester police station. He didn't even come home first. He wanted to get this mess all cleared up with the police and thought he would be in and out of the station, answer a few questions and come home with the unused computer in hand.

But hours passed, and he still wasn't home. Eventually I got a call from Harry at the station.

"Sarn, they are keeping me in," he said.

"What for? What is going on Harry?"

He explained how the police were investigating possible corruption involved in a player transfer. They were looking at a £100,000 payment made to a Portsmouth player, Amdy Faye, by his football agent Willie McKay back in 2003 when Harry was the manager. The police believed the money had been paid to avoid tax and wanted to know who gave the payment the green light – Harry being one of the suspects.

"I don't deal with the money side of things, Sarn," he said. "It is just a misunderstanding, it will all be sorted out soon."

A misunderstanding, I thought. I have had the police turn my house upside down, the whole road woken up by police cars – God only knows what our neighbours think – and the whole thing was being shown live on breakfast television. I was angry and embarrassed.

But above all of that, I knew Harry and trusted him. Harry wouldn't have been involved in anything like that. If anything, he is useless with money and relies on me or the accountant to sort out our finances. I remember years ago when our son Mark had a spell as a football agent and he had Rio Ferdinand on his books, and Harry wasn't happy. Rio played for Harry at West Ham, and there was no way Harry was going to negotiate a player's pay with his own son as their agent – how bad would that have looked? Harry told Mark it wasn't happening and in the end Rio had to find another agent. It meant Mark lost out on looking after Rio, but that is how serious Harry was about doing things right and by the book.

After a night in the cells, being questioned by police, Harry eventually arrived home. I was furious that things were in such a mess, but I hugged him so tightly when he walked through the door. Harry said he had told the police everything he knew and that it was nothing to do with him, and he isn't the one who pays the agent their fees. He also disclosed all of his finances to help the police with their investigations, including an account he had over in Monaco. Little did we know that Harry's honesty about the account would lead the police onto the path of another investigation. Our nightmare was only just beginning.

Chapter 22

On trial

'The wait for the verdict was awful. It felt like the jury was deliberating for weeks. Sandra was in bits at home, wanting to know if I was going home that night or if she was going to be visiting me in prison'

Harry

In May 2008, six months after the police tore into our house before sunrise and frightened the life out of poor Sandra, the police were told their actions were unlawful. Furious about their behaviour and conduct, particularly towards my wife, we launched a court challenge against the City of London Police, which went to the High Court. It was ruled a search of our home was unlawful and they were ordered to pay our legal costs. But it wasn't about the money, I couldn't care less about the legal costs. That meant nothing to me. It was the principle.

That house raid should never have happened and I wanted them to admit they were wrong.

Lord Justice Latham told the High Court the warrant was 'wholly unacceptable' and added, 'The obtaining of a search warrant is never to be treated as a formality. It authorises the invasion of a person's home.'

I can't say Sandra and I were thrilled. Of course, we were pleased that the judge agreed with us that the raid shouldn't have happened, but the whole thing had been a nightmare. The raid, my arrest, the night in the cells – that has to be one of the worst nights of my life – and then the High Court challenge. None of that came without stress. But as I say, it was the principle – we were fighting for what we knew was right.

Outside court, our solicitor, Mark Spragg, said, "This was an outrageous abuse of power by the police who ignored the rule book and executed an unlawful search warrant at 6am in the full glare of media coverage, which they no doubt organised or at least did not discourage."

The police denied tipping off the papers – an investigation showed a police officer had made calls to *The Sun* to invite the staff to a Christmas party. If that is what they say, then that is what they say, but I know what I think of the whole thing.

Sadly, the High Court ruling wasn't the end of my experience with the police. In fact, it was only just beginning. It turned out that after I disclosed an account I had in Monaco, a whole new investigation had started – and would result in my 2012 trial for tax evasion. Sandra was beside herself. It broke my heart how upset she was. But even though I knew she was angry, we never had an argument about it. You couldn't have a row with Sandra if you tried. If you got upset about something, she would say, "Look at you, calm down." She is so placid and so easy going. And we've always said throughout our marriage that you can't just have a row, and throw the towel in. You'll have good days and bad days and you just have to work through it. Though if I am honest, I wasn't sure how I was going to get through this trial, I was just glad I had Sandra's love and support and her by my side.

The Monaco account came about when I took over as director of football at Portsmouth. Milan Mandaric was the chairman and wanted to cut me a deal.

"I have Graham Rix as manager and I want you to come in as a consultant," Milan told me. "But I can't pay you much in wages, Harry."

I had left my job at West Ham, but I was still getting paid because I had a year left on my contract.

I knew Milan from America. When I was over there early on in my career, he was managing the San Jose team. He was the biggest owner in America and he was only in his 30s. He was so rich and was a businessman of the year out there. But still, he couldn't pay me a full wage.

"I'll tell you what I'll do," he said. "I'll give you a percentage of any players you bring in that we buy and when we sell them, I'll give you a profit."

They only sold one of the players I had brought in and that was Peter Crouch, but by the time Crouchy leaves, I am now the manager.

"You owe me the money from Peter Crouch," I told Milan.

"No, no Harry, you are the manager now. You have a different contract," he said.

"Yeah, but when we bought him, I was the director of football and you owe me," I shot back.

"No, no, no," he said. "I can't do it, you have a contract and we can't change that. I can't pay you now. It is not legal to pay you now. It is impossible. You have a new contract and it is not in that contract."

We ended up having an almighty argument and I nearly walked out of the club and I have only just taken over as manager.

He said, "Look, what I am going to do is give you some shares. I will put the money in and if there is a profit, you can have it. I have got some good shares coming."

"I don't want the profit on shares," I told him. "I just want my bonus, that is what you owe me."

Anyway, in the end, I tired of arguing. I wasn't going to get my bonus, and while I didn't want the profit of the shares, it was better than nothing.

"I want you to go to the bank in Monaco where I bank and I want you to meet the bank manager, and open an account," he said. "I will put some money in, base money, we can buy the shares and then you take the profit. If the shares are no good, you don't lose, but they will be good. Don't worry Harry, I'll make you more money than your bonus."

So then me and Sandra go to Monaco. We have never been before. We get to the hotel, have a bit of dinner and then the next morning Milan has arranged for me to meet this bank manager.

I go in and meet him – he is an Englishman, a big Fulham fan.

"Hello Harry, how are you?" he said. "Milan is putting some money in the account and he is going to buy some shares. We just need a password so that if anyone rings up we know it is your account."

I needed to think of a password on the spot, so I thought of Rosie, she was our old bulldog and I knew I would remember that.

And that was it, Sandra and I went off around Monaco for a few days, we had a lovely holiday, and we heard nothing from the bank. A year or 14 months have rolled by and I have still heard nothing.

By this point Portsmouth were facing a relegation battle, but we have won three on the spin, including beating our rivals Southampton at home, and we've just won 2-0 against Blackburn. We are staying up.

After the game, Milan comes up to me while I am chatting with Jim Smith and Kevin Bond and he can't stop cuddling me.

"Harry I love you, I can't thank you for what you have done for me, what you have done for this club," he says. "Come and have a glass of wine with me, let's go and celebrate."

I thought this was a good opportunity to ask about those shares. There has been radio silence for months and I want to know what is going on with them.

"Yeah, sorry Harry. It was a disaster," he said.

"Oh, really?" I replied.

"Yeah. I lost millions," he said. "It has been a disaster, Harry, a disaster. But listen don't worry, I am going to put some more money in and we will try again. Leave it with me."

I go back to see Jim and Kevin, and by now I have got the right hump.

"What is the matter?" Jim says, so I tell them the story.

Jim says to me, "Harry, are you mad? Do you think he ever put any money in there in the first place?"

"Of course he did," I said. "He told me he put the money in there." Jim still wasn't convinced.

About 18 months later I got a new accountant, a fella called Malcolm, and while I am going through all my accounts, I tell him the story about Monaco. But I couldn't remember the name of the bank. I told you I am rubbish with financial stuff.

"Alan Hills is a manager with HSBC and he worked in Monaco for 12 years," Malcolm said. "He might know."

Malcolm gets to the bottom of it and finds out it was HSBC in Monaco and there is about £10,000 in the account. Milan must have put some more money in there for shares, I thought.

"Draw it out, Harry," Malcolm said. "It is your money, draw it out." So I did.

The next thing I knew, I was being arrested by the police as they suspect it is money that has been used in a transfer or something. I was then charged with two counts of cheating the public revenue. Milan faced the same. This was getting serious, but I was innocent. I have never evaded tax in my life, and I was adamant I was going to clear my name, so I got the best barrister in the country, John Kelsey Fry, a recommendation from my friend Michael. He told me, "You might think you're crushing a walnut with a sledgehammer Harry, but you can't take chances. Go and see John Kelsey Fry."

And that was the best advice I have ever taken. He was absolutely fantastic. "What will happen if I am found guilty?" I asked him.

"You might get three years," he said. Three years? I hadn't done anything wrong.

The court case was a joke when it shouldn't have been. And I mean literally full of jokes.

On trial

At one point, Milan stood up in court and said, "Yeah, I woke up one morning and I said to my manager Harry, I am bored, I have paid 100 million in income tax and you've paid nine million in income tax, but I know, why don't we see if we can fiddle things for £10k." He was obviously taking the mickey, but that was how ludicrous the case was.

Everyone also got a laugh during the jury selection. Milan and I were sitting behind the glass on the first day of the trial when 24 people walked in. They drew out numbers one by one, then they got to juror number six.

The clerk said, "Juror number six is Peter Crouch." There is a geezer who was six foot seven, as skinny as a rake with blonde hair walking towards the jury box. The court bursts out laughing, including me and Milan. I had to laugh otherwise I would have probably cried.

Not only is this fella a ringer for Crouchy – if you were picking somebody to play Peter Crouch in a film you would pick this man – but the case is called the Peter Crouch Bonus case. You couldn't make it up.

We adjourn for lunch at 2pm, and when we come back the clerk is having a quiet word with the judge. The judge then says that a national newspaper has tweeted about Peter the juror and now the whole jury needs to be dismissed and reselected. And that was it, Peter Crouch was off the jury. And the other funny thing was, Peter Crouch the juror was only a steward at Tottenham. I mean what are the chances?

But for the most part, the trial wasn't funny. It was deadly serious and if this jury thought me and Milan had done something wrong, we were looking at going to prison. I could only think of Sandra. I couldn't let her come to court with me. I couldn't give evidence with her at the back – I would have broken down. I know she would have broken down too. Early on we decided she was going to stay at home with Mark, and Jamie was going to come to court with me every day.

One of the worst points for me, and one that I am glad Sandra didn't witness, was when I gave my evidence. Detective Inspector David Manley of the City of London Police was in court to hear my evidence. He hadn't been in court for the whole trial, but he turned up that day. I knew why. He wasn't nice to me at all throughout the whole investigation, and he let it be known he didn't like me as he sat at the back of the court staring at me. As I was being cross-examined by Mr Black, I could see Mr Manley's eyes burning into me. He had a real cocky look on his face. He just glared at me, and I don't think he blinked. I lost my train of thought.

"Your Honour," I said. "Mr Manley is intimidating me and I can't concentrate."

"I know, I can see that," he said. "Mr Manley, either move your seat or leave the court."

I don't know what his problem was, but I could tell he wanted me to be found guilty.

The wait for the verdict was awful. It felt like the jury was deliberating for weeks. Sandra was in bits at home, wanting to know if I was going home that night or if she was going to be visiting me in prison.

When the foreman of the jury finally gave the verdict, I felt like I had won every football title you can think of. Of course I knew I was innocent, but there was that chance the jury might not believe me and now everyone – every fan who has said a bad word in the stands, every journalist who has written about me, and Mr Manley, the man who tried to intimidate me – knew I was not guilty. 'I can finally get my life back,' I thought.

Looking back on it now, it really was a scary time for us and all over nothing. The worst thing I ever did was to take the money out. I paid it back to Milan as it was his money and I never did get my bonus. I had five years of grief and I never got my bloody bonus!

"Why don't we go for a drink, Dad, we need to celebrate," Jamie said as we walked down the steps of Southwark Crown Court.

"Nah, I want to get home to your mum," I told him. Grabbing my shoulder, Jamie smiled knowingly. "Okay, let's go home, Dad," he said.

"Have you heard the news, Harry?" a reporter shouted at me from across the road.

"No, what has happened?" I asked.

"Capello's resigned!" came the reply.

'Wow,' I thought. I feel like this was meant to happen. Perhaps things were starting to look good again.

Chapter 23

Life is too short

'Harry and I flew over to spend some time with them. We had been having a lovely week, but I could tell there was something different about my brother – he didn't look or seem his usual self'

Sandra

Harry's trial was no doubt one of the biggest tests of our marriage. The whole thing lasted for five years and was like a dark cloud hanging over us. We felt like we couldn't really enjoy anything. Every time we went out for dinner, I would worry that people were looking at us and talking. What were people thinking?

Harry wanted it all over, and I did too. The stress of waiting for the court case was too much. Part of me was annoyed with Harry for getting into the situation in the first place, even though of course he didn't do anything wrong. But the most part of me felt so sorry for him. I was worried sick at the thought of Harry going to prison. What if the jury doesn't believe him?

I tried my hardest to be strong for Harry, but I think he knew that deep down I was in pieces. I think that's why he wouldn't let me go to court every day with him, and why he took Jamie instead. He didn't want me to see him in the dock and put me through even more stress than I had already been through. I think he was also secretly worried about going to prison too, and he wouldn't have wanted me to know he was terrified.

When Harry was acquitted, it finally felt like a weight had been lifted from us. I felt relieved, but also annoyed that it ever went to trial in the first place. I saw a change in Harry; he could start living his life again.

The whole thing was a horrible nightmare for us both, and probably one of the worst things to happen to me after losing my parents and siblings.

My brother Brian was one of the nicest men you could meet. He was a bit of a gentle giant – stocky and broad, but very quiet.

I remember Brian introducing us to his girlfriend, Barbara, for the first time. Me, my sister Pat and her then boyfriend Frank had arranged to meet them at our local pub and when we walked in I remember seeing them both laughing together.

As we approached their table, Brian spotted us and stood up, towering over me and Pat like he always did.

"This is Barbara," he said softly.

"Hello darlings!" she said, giving us air kisses.

Barbara seemed nice. As a teenager myself, I remember thinking how flamboyant and glamorous she was in her faux fur coat. She was also louder than Brian.

He was a shy man, but he and Barbara seemed to click. Pat and I wondered if they would work as they seemed to be like chalk and cheese. And when Barbara came running out of the pub toilets screaming her head off as she had seen a spider, Pat and I looked at each other and gave a little smile. But it just goes to show that opposites can attract. In fact, Brian and Barbara had a long and happy marriage, with two children, a son Richard, and daughter, Sam.

They got married in a registry office the year before me and Harry. And me and Pat had more in common with Barbara than we first thought as she was a hairdresser too!

They first moved into Barbara's flat in Dagenham before following the Harris family tradition of buying a house in Barking. Later in their marriage, they bought an apartment in Spain and moved over there to live.

Harry and I would visit them as often as we could and they'd come and see us in Bournemouth.

In October, Harry and I flew over to spend some time with them. We had been having a lovely week, but I could tell there was something different about my brother – he didn't look or seem his usual self.

One night we went out for dinner, just the four of us.

"Erm, I think I will have the risotto please?" Brian said.

'Risotto?' I thought. What an odd choice. I don't think I had ever seen my brother go to a restaurant and not order a steak.

When our food arrived, I could see him pushing it around the plate with a fork.

"Are you okay?" I asked, but Brian assured me he was fine.

Harry and I had only been back home in Bournemouth for a couple of weeks, when Barbara called.

"I have some news," she said. "Brian has cancer of the oesophagus."

"Oh my goodness!" I said. "That is why he was eating risotto!"

"He hasn't been able to digest food properly for a while," Barbara said. "But they are going to operate and I have told him he is going to be fine. We need to stay positive."

I was amazed by how strong Barbara was, but she has always been someone who is glass half full.

Years ago, she was involved in a terrible car accident close to a flower shop she owned in Sawbridgeworth. She had a head-on collision and had to have a lot of surgery – yet she was always positive. So we couldn't think of anyone better to be by Brian's side as he went through surgery.

Before he went down, she took him by his face and told him it would all be okay – not just to make him feel better, but because she truly believed it.

And when he had his operation and the doctors opened him up, realised the cancer had spread and that his prognosis wasn't good, Barbara was so amazing.

She is quite a spiritual person and I think that is where she gets her strength from. She is into crystals and crystal healing, and will visit a clairvoyant every now and then, and I think that helps her remain positive – even in the worst of circumstances.

Brian died at the age of 68, just months after being diagnosed. Cancer is cruel, and cancer of the oesophagus is just awful. It took him so quickly.

And there was more devastating news to come. Two years after losing Brian, there was further heartache when his son Richard died following a heart attack. It was totally out of the blue. And again, Barbara was so strong. I can't ever imagine losing Harry. Losing your husband must be awful, but to also lose your baby – you don't expect your children to go before you.

We have remained in touch with Barbara. She is still in Spain and she is happy there. And she is as upbeat as ever. You'll never see her down. I admire her in many ways. We've had terrible losses in our family, people who we've loved gone way too soon, but death always makes you realise that there is life. And life is too short.

Chapter 24

England calling

'Football is what I love, it is my passion and that is my way of showing it sometimes. Maybe the FA didn't like that approach or style of management, but who knows?'

Harry

One of my biggest ambitions during my career was to be the England manager. It is the dream of any English manager, and they are lying if they say it's not. We'd had many years of foreign coaches looking after the Three Lions, but for me, it would have been an absolute honour as an Englishman.

Sadly for me, it never happened. Though I got close. Very close.

After hearing that Fabio Capello had resigned on the morning I had been found not guilty of tax evasion, my phone started ringing off the hook.

"Harry, this job is yours, surely," my mates would say. "You've got to be first choice, the only choice." Apparently, I was the people's choice, too.

And for the first time ever, as a gambling man, even I thought I had a bit of a chance.

I think Sandra was worried about it. She knows how seriously I take my job, and I think she was quite worried about the extra pressure being the England manager would bring. Obviously, she doesn't like it when I am down, and she thought taking the job might be a bit much. But Sandra has always been my biggest supporter. Any worries have come about because she cares, and, ultimately, I know she would back me whatever I decided.

It was very strange timing for me. It felt as though Capello thought 'Harry's not going to prison, he has been found not guilty, he is going to get the England job, I think I'll resign today.'

Of course, that wasn't really what happened, but it was strange. Almost like fate.

I was at Spurs at the time, and things were going well, we had a good team and were getting results. And I was happy there, really happy. But the England job was something I couldn't ever turn down and the Spurs chairman, Daniel Levy, always knew that if the FA came knocking, I would want to talk to them.

But while this was the dream job for me, I wasn't silly – I knew what came with it. As soon as you are announced as the England manager, there are people ready to dig you out. There have been some really nice people over the years who have been destroyed by being the England manager. Bobby Robson got almighty grief at one time and Graham Taylor got slaughtered. He was a nice man and a good manager.

It was a poisoned chalice, but in all honesty, I was ready to take it on.

I had some people at the FA who I knew were backing me and people from the League Managers Association. "The job is yours, Harry," they'd say. "They will want you."

Me and Roy Hodgson seemed to be the only two in the running – and it was eventually Roy who got the job.

I don't know what happened, really. I had this crazy clause in my contract which meant that if another club came after me – or in this case the FA – they would have to pay £5million back to Portsmouth, the last club I was at before Spurs, plus all my wages for my time at Tottenham and whatever was left on my contract. It was looking like a £15million buy-out clause. The contract was done when I wasn't there, and I only knew how much they would pay me if they sacked me – that was a £1million payout – but I was clueless as to the consequences if I were to go elsewhere. It is mad when you think about it – a million if I am sacked, but the club would get £15million if I broke my contract and went to another club.

Knowing how to show a girl a good time! Mixing with royalty – in this case Prince Charles – at a Prince's Trust event at St James's Palace

Sea legs One of the advantages of living near the coast is getting to enjoy the maritime life. Here we are onboard a yacht at Cowes Powerboat Racing Weekend in 2019

Handsome couple! There's been a lot more attention on us since Harry went on *I'm A Celebrity* but life is a lot more relaxed and enjoyable

Holiday snap Here we are in beautiful Greece, soaking up the sun

Happy together We've seen a few big occasions in nearly 60 years as a couple – but we don't usually mark them with candles in a lasagne!

Scrubbing up well With lots of lovely friends, there are plenty of big celebrations to dress up for, like jungle camp-mate James McVey's wedding in 2021

Christmas jumpers Every year I pretend I've forgotten to get Sarn a Christmas present, and every year I surprise her with something... at least I think it's still a surprise!

What do they say about dogs and their owners? No house is complete without man's best friend. Here is our current dog Barney, an English bulldog

Next generation Harry and three of our grandchildren (pictured from left to right) Bobbie, Harry Jnr and Charley

A ray of sunshine Having boys was wonderful but when our granddaughter Molly came along, it was lovely to have a girl in the family

Generation game
Here we are with grandson Joe, great grandson Hendrix and Joe's partner Anoushka

Nanny and Pop
It's wonderful being grandparents to our eight grandkids – they keep us on our toes, that's for sure!

Happy memories
Mark's wife Lucy on her wedding day with Harry and her dad, Bob

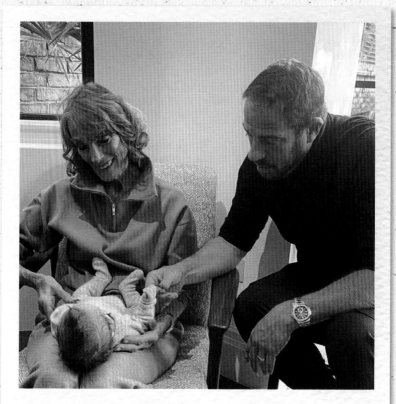

Doting Nanny
Mark and I stare at Jamie's son, baby Rafa, just before Christmas 2021

Happy new arrival
Posing for a picture with Jamie's wife Frida and baby Rafa

My boy Jamie amazes me when I watch him now on TV as a football pundit, he speaks so well and uses words I don't understand. I think, 'But you didn't really go to school! You went to training with your dad!'

Fit to fly Arriving in Australia to see Harry after spending weeks apart

Christmas with the Redknapps With Jamie, Frida, Charley, Beau and Raphael

King of the jungle For some reason the nation kept voting to keep me in until there was no-one else left. I ended up winning *I'm A Celebrity* and our lives have changed ever since

I didn't look at the finer print, I never have, and that is my fault and I should have done. It was a crazy clause, all in Tottenham's favour, but what could I do? I suppose that is what you get for not reading your contract properly.

I am not saying that is the reason why the FA didn't go for me, but I think it is a possibility. The FA have certainly never said that, but they have also never said why they chose not to ask me for an interview.

I had heard what people were saying about my relationship with Sir Trevor Brooking, the FA's director of football development, and the fact that we had never seen eye to eye and how that could have contributed to me not getting the job. I know that there are people who think he has never forgiven me for taking over from Billy Bonds at West Ham, but I don't believe that. I refuse to believe that. First of all, he is not a spiteful man in the slightest and besides, he wasn't at the club at the time I took over. I was also invited to his wedding and he came to my dad's funeral. I can't say we were ever the best of friends, that is being honest, but I don't believe for one second that he would have got in the way of me and the England job. He would have had to turn the whole board against me, and what was he going to say to do that? I just don't buy it.

I just think I would have worked out very expensive for the FA and Roy would have been a cheaper option. I am not having a pop at Roy by the way, or running him down. I think he is a decent fella with great experience. I just think he was probably a bit more of the FA's cup of tea than I ever was. Roy was coached by the FA from a young age after packing football in as a player. He would have always gone on courses, getting his badges and qualifications, and he probably knew more about what they want from a manager. I am not sure the FA are that keen on managers who are a bit rough around the edges, like me. I have an opinion and I am not afraid to get tough with people and give them a kick up the backside if they need it. I am not afraid to lose it on the touchline or say what I think in a post-match interview. Football is what I love, it is my passion and that is my way of showing it sometimes. Maybe the FA didn't like that approach or style of management, but who knows?

That was my time, really, if I was going to get it. It was then or never for me.

"Everything happens for a reason, Harry," Sandra said to me.

"But that was my last chance to be England manager," I said, kicking myself in frustration that I didn't question the contract at the time.

"It will work out," she said. "You've still got a job that you love." And as always, Sandra was right. Spurs were sitting fourth in the league and were looking to claim a Champions League place.

Would I have taken the England job if it was offered to me again, years down the line? No. I really believe if I was ever going to be England manager, that would have been my one and only opportunity. If I had been offered it after Roy, or after that, no, I wouldn't have taken it. I would have taken my hat out of the ring before the speculation had even started in the papers and on Sky Sports News. I would have called up TalkSport personally to rule myself out.

I still have an opinion on the England team, even now, any Englishman into football does. Gareth Southgate is an absolutely fantastic manager and he has a very good team under him. Harry Kane is fantastic, what a player.

And by saying I wouldn't have taken the job after that time is not me cutting my nose off to spite my face, it is just me knowing that period of my life was the perfect time to take on the job.

But, as I say, it wasn't meant to be. And I knew that because I didn't lose sleep over it. I was frustrated, yes, I was kicking myself over that bloody contract, yes, but I didn't get that deep depression that I have felt before during my career. I didn't feel that I needed to cut myself off from people, it didn't leave me feeling low.

I phoned Roy to congratulate him when he was announced as the manager in May 2012. There were no hard feelings and I told him I hoped he did well. I also told him I hoped people would be kind to him, because it really is a tough job being a manager, let alone the England manager.

Chapter 25

Run over by my husband

'All of a sudden I felt this huge pressure on my foot and I was suddenly being dragged down. 'Harry!!' I screamed. I started banging on the car'

Sandra

"I just hope I don't embarrass myself or my family," came a familiar voice from the TV.

"As if she would embarrass us!" I told Harry as we both watched our daughter-in-law Louise on screen. It was August 2016 and we were watching her on the Matthew Wright show. She had just been announced as the sixth contestant on that year's *Strictly Come Dancing*.

Louise was excited and nervous, but couldn't wait to get stuck into training. She had raised both her and Jamie's boys,

Charley and Beau, and hadn't really done anything for herself since she was in Eternal. She had been offered *Strictly* a few times over the years and had always turned it down. But this year she went for it, and I think she wanted to get out and try something new.

"Jamie has got zero rhythm, he is mortified!" she said. "I am hoping he'll be proud."

"Course he will, Lou," Harry said to the TV.

Harry doesn't watch much TV, well not unless, of course, it is football or horse racing, but he does like *Strictly*, and it is one of my favourite programmes too, besides the soaps. I love the *Strictly* music, the costumes and the old school dancing. I couldn't wait to go and see her on the show.

When September came around, I couldn't wait to get to the studio each week with Jamie and Louise's mum, Lynne. She was a lovely lady and we got on really well.

Louise had been partnered with Kevin Clifton – he had quite a good track record as a professional and was a great dancer, so I was really hoping they would win.

But just a few weeks into the series, I had an accident which meant I could no longer go to the *Strictly* studio. An accident that literally took me off my feet.

I have had a lot of knocks and bumps over the years. There was the time I fractured two ankle bones. There was the night I broke my ankle going to a show to see my then daughter-in-law

Louise in concert. I was walking down a winding staircase and the next thing I knew, my heel got caught and I fell down the stairs. But I didn't realise how badly I had hurt myself. That night I came home, went to bed and it was only when I woke up the next morning and my ankle had blown up that I thought I had better get it checked out – it turned out I had broken it.

Then there was the time I slipped and broke my coccyx bone in the garden. In our old house we had a dip in the ground, it was at a 45-degree angle. I had watered the garden earlier that day and, forgetting it was still wet, I shot down the astro turf like it was a slide. I was on my own that day and had to crawl into the house to get help. I still don't know how I managed it.

There was another time when I fell over the pavement and my foot went underneath me. I managed to call Molly's mum Rachel, and she came and scooped me off the pavement.

"I am alright," I told her.

"No, you are not, we are going to get your foot looked at," she told me.

To be honest, it was lucky I did listen and go to the hospital as my foot had been bent completely back the other way.

"It is like you have been on a motorbike and your foot has been dragged backwards," the doctor told me.

I had to sit for six weeks until it went into plaster and I wasn't a very good patient as I don't like sitting around. I remember Rachel used to cook me fish fingers, mash and grilled tomatoes.

Run over by my husband

And then there was the day I got run over by my husband. Before I tell this story, I have to say I don't blame Harry at all. I might joke with him that it was "another mess Mr Pastry has got me into", but all I cared about was that he was okay. I knew the whole thing had traumatised him so badly and I was so upset that he was upset.

We were driving to Westbourne, a little village about five miles from our house in Sandbanks. There is a one-way system and there were cars parked either side. You could probably just get a bus through the road. Harry saw a space and pulled into it so I could pop into the shops.

"Don't get out Sarn, there is a car coming," Harry told me. I waited for the car to go by and then jumped out, making my way around to the back of the car, so I could wait to cross safely. But the traffic didn't stop, so I came back and waited.

Then all of a sudden I felt this huge pressure on my foot and I was suddenly being dragged down.

"Harry!!" I screamed. I started banging on the car. "Harry!!" He had reversed over my ankle. He had checked his wing mirror to see if he was clear, and thinking I had gone, moved the car backwards.

I fell into the road as a bus was coming. I could just hear Harry panicking. Out of nowhere my friend Joanne appeared and I could hear her voice.

"Don't look at her foot, Harry," she said. "Harry, are you listening? Please don't look at it."

The next thing I remember is sirens and being stretchered into the back of an ambulance.

"I won't be able to go to *Strictly* this weekend," I told the paramedic. "I need to be well enough to go." Harry's reaction was very different – he had a look of panic on his face.

"Sarn, what have I done? Sarn, I am so sorry," he said. I could see he was distraught. "It is okay," I reassured him. "It was just an accident."

"Would you like some gas and air?" the paramedic asked, though from the look on Harry's face, he probably needed it more than me!

I took the pump and started inhaling, hoping the pain would ease. Even before I had any gas and air I felt strangely calm – it was Harry who was beside himself and in a panic, and it was breaking my heart to see him in such a state.

"I thought I took your foot off, Sarn," he said. "I thought I had lost you!"

Suddenly, out of nowhere, our granddaughter Molly appeared in the back of the ambulance. At first, I thought it was the gas and air, but it was really Molly. She had been on a bus going to work and held up in the traffic caused by the accident. She had seen me being stretchered into the ambulance and asked the driver to let her off the bus. It breaks my heart that she saw that. It must have been awful for her to see me like that, and I could tell she was also worried.

"What has happened, Pop?" she asked Harry. But he couldn't find the words. "Pop, what is going on?"

"I have sliced her foot into pieces, Mol," he told her. "It is a horrible mess. Half her foot was hanging out in the road."

Harry wasn't making any sense and as we made our way to the hospital, the paramedic explained to Molly what had happened while I was enjoying the effects of the gas and air. It wasn't long before the press had got wind of the accident and there were photographers camped outside the hospital.

'Redknapp runs over wife in freak accident' was one headline; another read 'Harry Redknapp runs over wife and drags her along the street'. Harry was traumatised.

Then, to make matters worse, we had a visit from the police – I suppose they needed to make sure Harry hadn't committed a crime. Though if you read the papers, you would think otherwise – they were taking photographs of the blood like it was a crime scene! Luckily, the officers were as good as gold.

After an operation on the foot, it was put into a cast and I was sent home on crutches. Harry picked me up as I was wheeled to the car – in a Primark white dressing gown with pink hearts, no less! This was my worst nightmare, not because of the accident, but I was on the front pages!

Once home, I received flowers and lots of lovely cards from well-wishers – well, mainly well-wishers – one card read 'He did it on purpose!' We still laugh about that now.

I ended up having skin grafts as the injury kept getting infected, but it has actually healed quite well. Sometimes it might flare up if I exercise, but I was lucky. Harry says I am like a cat with nine lives.

I always say what doesn't kill you makes you stronger. I have been through enough in my life to know that. And I know it sounds a bit cheesy, but I am a born survivor – I almost didn't make it when I came into the world.

And I don't want sympathy or people feeling sorry for me either, as I really don't want to make a big deal out of it. The accident was so easily done. You only have to switch off for a second.

I remember there was a girl in my class at school, and she had a distorted face because her dad reversed the car and it hit her. He accidentally ruined her beautiful face and had to live with that regret his whole life. People ask why I haven't given Harry more stick, but I would never do that to him. He was totally devastated by the whole accident and won't ever forgive himself. I don't need to forgive him, though, as I wouldn't ever blame him for it.

Chapter 26

Shock news and absent friends

'Sandra was right. I could feel something in my body and I knew it wasn't right. I made a call to my doctor and within days I was given news that really shook me'

Harry

Sandra has had her fair share of trips and falls over the years – she is very accident-prone, is my wife. And then there was the day I ran her over. My God, that has got to be one of the worst days of my life. I panicked when I jumped out of the car. I thought another car had hit her. I heard her scream, but I didn't realise it was me who'd knocked her down. I really thought for a moment in time that I had lost her. She was lying in absolute agony on the floor, yet so calm. I looked down in horror at her foot, which looked like it had been sliced like a piece of bacon. There was blood everywhere. And it was all my fault.

The next thing I know, our granddaughter Molly was in front of me asking if I was okay. I couldn't speak. Sandra has never blamed me for it. She is unbelievable. Even when she was lying on the floor she never said, "You should have watched what you were doing" or made me feel bad about it. She is incredible.

She has also been through some periods of ill health in her life when she has had to have a few operations, and she has always been so strong. Sandra's a very positive person and is amazingly calm, even when I am not!

When I had an operation on my knee in 2015 and ended up on crutches, Sandra looked after me around the clock.

And then there was my cancer scare back in 2016. I'll never forget how amazing Sandra was during what was probably the worst and most terrifying of all my health scares.

I had agreed to become Derby County's director of football for the remainder of the 2015/16 season, but first I agreed to take a brief job managing Jordan's national team for a couple of games while they prepared for their qualifiers for the 2018 World Cup, which was being held in Russia.

The job came about as I was friends with Jordanian football chief Prince Ali bin Hussein and he had asked me to oversee their game against Bangladesh in Amman and another against Australia down in Sydney.

I knew it was going to be a tough couple of weeks, but I missed the buzz of football.

We thrashed Bangladesh 8-0. It was an incredible win and everyone was on a high, including me. Next up was a trip Down Under to face the Group B favourites. Sadly, they thumped us 5-1. But Jordan were an alright team and came second in the group. My work was done.

I was on my way back from Australia when I suddenly felt very ill. My old mate and long-term work colleague Kevin Bond was with me after joining me to be Jordan's assistant coach. We were breaking up the journey home with a stop in Dubai, but Kevin took one look at me and said, "There is no way you can get on that connecting plane. Look at you!"

"No, I have got to get home to Sandra," I told him. "I want to get home."

Against Kevin's advice, I got on the plane and I think I slept the whole way home.

Back on UK soil, and back home with Sandra, I told her what had happened.

"You need to go to the doctor and get it looked at Harry," she said to me calmly.

"It is probably nothing, but it won't hurt to get it checked."

Sandra always says the right things in bad situations. And she was right, I did need to go. I could feel something in my body and I knew it wasn't right. I made a call to my doctor and within days I was given news that really shook me.

"You have a tumour on your bladder, Mr Redknapp," the consultant told me. "We need to remove it urgently."

I was terrified. Like anyone would hearing those words, I feared the worst. I wanted it out of me. I wanted to go back to how things were a few months ago. I wanted to get back into the buzz of football. I wanted to be at home with Sandra and the dog.

The day of the operation, I felt sick. You will have heard of pre-match nerves, but it was like nothing I had ever experienced before. How big was this tumour going to be? What else are they going to find? What happens if anything goes wrong?

The doctors removed the tumour and sent it off for tests. It felt like time wasn't going quickly enough. After a couple of days I was up and about on my feet and was recovering well, but the results were still hanging over me.

Then the news came.

"I am pleased to tell you the mass was benign," the consultant said to me.

"Benign?" I asked. "Do you mean..."

"Yes, there is no sign of cancer, Mr Redknapp," he said. "You have the all clear. However, I would like you to come for check-ups every three months, just so we can keep an eye on you."

I let out a huge sigh of relief. I felt like a huge weight had been lifted from my shoulders.

Looking back, it was a frightening time. I really thought the tumour would kill me. But now I am a lot more relaxed about these things, because life is short and what can we do about it? Sandra and I are in our mid-seventies now and when you get to a certain age, you do start to get ill and have health issues. We have lost many close family and friends over the years – most of them taken far too young – but unfortunately, that is life, isn't it? As cruel as it is.

Sandra and I have been through our own scares over the years, and we have both been very lucky and fortunate to have come out the other side, and we know others haven't. That is why we have to be grateful for what we have and live each day. Sandra always says "what doesn't kill you makes you stronger" and she is right. Life really is too short.

February 24, 2018 marked 25 years since my great friend Bobby Moore died.

It is hard to believe that so much time has passed since his untimely death. I could cry thinking about him. I loved Bobby to pieces. He was an absolutely fantastic fella and a brilliant footballer, one of the best there will ever be.

Bobby was someone I always looked up to from the day I met him. I was young when I joined West Ham, and he was older and experienced, and he just took me under his wing.

And it was a theme throughout our friendship, as he always looked after and guided me. In 1979, when he was made manager of Oxford City, he took me there as his assistant. But some of our best memories were when we were in America together. Sandra and Tina grew close and got on really well. She was as fond of Bobby as I was, and my boys looked up to him and absolutely idolised him, too.

After we won the World Cup in 1966, Bobby became the most famous person in the world. The picture of him holding the Jules Rimet trophy as he was lifted up by Geoff Hurst and Ray Wilson in the middle of the victorious team at Wembley Stadium became iconic. It even became a statue. But to me, he was just Bobby. He was my friend – he was a normal, down to earth guy. His wife Tina was the same. A lot of people see them as the power couple of the 60s and there was a TV series based on their relationship a few years ago, based on Tina's autobiography, but Bobby would have laughed at that.

"What would they want to make a drama series out of me and Tina for?" he would say if he was still with us today.

Bobby was a very shy man, but he came out of his shell a bit more after a couple of lagers. I remember one time we were out having dinner and a couple of fans approached the table and asked Bobby to dance. He accepted, and as he walked past Tina, she threw her gin and tonic all over him. Bobby dabbed his finger in the drink and said, "Can I have a touch more tonic?" Tina wasn't happy, but it was all a joke.

Bobby was actually very unassuming given his qualities and talent, and he certainly never realised how special he really was.

That is why it angered me so much when he was shunned by his own club because Bobby was one of the good guys of football. I was at Upton Park one day and I was sitting next to Frank Lampard Snr's mum, Hilda. All the family and friends of players would sit in E block and watch the game together – but Bobby wouldn't. He would go and sit up in a corner somewhere and watch. He didn't want to cause a commotion or a fuss. He would come into the ground just before kick-off and leave just before the final whistle – he just wanted to watch the game under the radar.

On this day, I caught Bobby coming into the ground. It was the year after we had come back from America, and we loved reminiscing and having a catch-up.

"Shall we have a cup of tea at half-time?" I asked him. Then out of nowhere a steward came up to us.

"Bobby, can I ask, do you have a ticket?" He looked a bit embarrassed and so he should have been. He was asking the captain of the World Cup-winning team if he had a ticket to watch a game at the club where he played more than 500 games. It is like Steven Gerrard being asked if he has a ticket to watch a game at Anfield.

"No, I don't," Bobby said, looking a bit confused.

"Well in that case, I'm really sorry Bobby, but I am going to have to ask you to leave," the steward said. "It hasn't come from me, it is the secretary," he quickly added.

I think my jaw probably hit the floor. I couldn't believe what I was witnessing. A West Ham hero turfed out of his old club.

John Lyall was the manager at the time, and I don't think he wanted Bobby in the ground. He took over from Ron Greenwood as manager, and I know Ron didn't approve of Bobby's lifestyle when he was his manager. Bobby wasn't the biggest drinker in the game, but he did like to have a few beers in the Black Lion pub the night before the game and sometimes after the game, and I don't think Ron liked that. But there was a drinking culture in football back then, and there were only a few who frowned upon it. I think when John took over, he wanted Bobby to keep his distance. Perhaps he felt threatened by Bobby and how big he was as a player, and maybe John didn't want him taking the attention away from him as a man-ager. Who knows? But the hypocrisy after Bobby died angered me. It still makes me sick to my stomach now that there is a Bobby Moore statue and a stand named after him, yet the club didn't care about him when he was alive. They want to sing and dance about the achievements of Bobby for his club and country now, but when he was alive they were kicking him out of the stadium. He wasn't even offered the opportunity to be a coach or an assistant manager. Imagine Bobby Moore training the youth team. Imagine the amount of players Bobby could have brought to the club if he had been there.

Bobby didn't expect anything from anyone and certainly wouldn't have expected the red carpet treatment at Upton Park, but I know that he lost himself when he retired. He lived and breathed football and then when he grew too old for the game, no one wanted to give him a job. Bobby fell into a depression and I saw him at some low points. He did lose his sparkle a bit. It makes me so angry that the last years of his life he spent feeling rejected by the game he loved the most.

Bobby first had a health scare when he was diagnosed with testicular cancer in 1964 when Tina was pregnant with their daughter Roberta. She was terrified she was going to lose him and begged the surgeons not to tell him he had cancer – but he recovered and went on to lift the World Cup just months later.

But no one ever knew there was far worse to come. Bobby was diagnosed with bowel and liver cancer in 1993, and a week after the world found out, he was gone. He was just 51. It was a terrible shock. I was absolutely heartbroken.

His funeral was held at Putney Vale Crematorium on March 2, which also happened to be my 46th birthday. There was a memorial service for him at Westminster Abbey a few months later and all the boys from the 1966 World Cup-winning team were there, as well as George Best, Bobby's

Fulham team-mate and another really fantastic footballer who was taken far too soon.

George was one of the best players I have ever seen. He was a genius, and very much like Bobby, he was very, very shy. And they had another similar quality in that they would come out of their shell after a drink.

George didn't really like the limelight. We would go racing together at Salisbury, just so he could be out of the way a bit and have a quiet day out. I remember one day we were leaving to go home and were driving up this country lane.

There were two blokes in their 50s walking up the lane.

"Look, Harry," he said. "It is us in the future." Then he let out a laugh.

"Why don't we ask them if they want a lift?" he said.

So we pull over and these two men jump in. "We are going to Fordingbridge," they say.

"No problem," says George. I don't think they could believe their luck, not only to get a lift four miles up a country lane, but to have George Best in the driving seat.

We get a bit further up and find another chap and George pulls over again. It was just the kind-hearted person George was.

I loved George, he was a great guy. Obviously he had a drink problem, but he wasn't ever an aggressive drunk, you know. I always found him to be very mellow.

Shock news and absent friends

I realised George had a problem with drink pretty early on, when he came down to play for Bournemouth in 1983. The following year he was arrested for drink driving, assaulting a police officer, and failing to answer bail and was given a three-month prison sentence – and ended spending that Christmas behind bars.

There was a very big drinking culture in football in those days and players used to drink after a game. It was only when the foreign players started to come to play in England, like Gianfranco Zola and Paolo Di Canio and they were super fit, that footballers drinking became a thing of the past. Well, for most.

Graeme Souness tells a great story about when he played at Sampdoria. They had played a pre-season game against a little non-league team and had thrashed them 8-0. All the players were getting on the coach, and Graeme stepped on with a bottle of Peroni in his hand. The next day, he got called in by the club's president.

"If that happens again, you are out," he told Graeme.

The Italian players, in particular, at that time really looked after themselves, while 90 per cent of the players here would be drinking after a game. It was a British thing, but also a football thing. I heard a story about a young player who didn't drink, but saw the other players drinking and thought, 'Well, they are okay'. So he took up drinking and then ended up having a problem with alcohol later in life. It also happened to Kenny

Sansom. He was such a lovely kid, very clean cut. He made his debut as a defender for Crystal Palace, his local club, when he was about 16, and I remember he was interviewed afterwards, saying how much he loved to play and loved the game. He was such a good player and went on to play for Arsenal, Newcastle, QPR and Everton. But then it all just went wrong for him – the drink, the gambling.

Kenny used to tell me how he would get his wage packet on a Friday – you'd get your wages in an envelope every week – and then he would have lost all his wages before he got home on a Friday night. Sixty quid gone on drink and gambling, a whole week's money.

To see the pictures of him in a newspaper sleeping rough on a park bench were just heartbreaking. But like all these players, or anyone who struggles with addiction, you have to be able to take the help when you are offered it and want to take it.

George didn't, sadly. He was diagnosed with severe liver damage in 2000 at the age of 54. His liver was only functioning at about 20 per cent and he went into hospital with pneumonia. Two years later he was given a liver transplant, a lifeline, and he even said in an interview with a newspaper that same year, "I was ill and everyone could see it but me." But he just couldn't give up the drink and died nearly four years later, aged 59. Another very brilliant footballer taken too soon, but at least the legacy they have both left won't ever be forgotten.

Shock news and absent friends

Bobby is buried about 20 yards away from my mum and dad in The City of London Cemetery on Aldersbrook Road in Wanstead. He had his funeral over in west London, as he lived there with his second wife, Stephanie Parlane, but he was brought back to the East End to be laid to rest. Every time I go to the crematorium to lay flowers for my mum and dad, I always take some to put on Bobby's plaque. Whenever I pull up in my car, the lady on the flower stall outside always recognises me and asks how I am doing. She knows exactly who I am there to see and will always check and ask if I know where I am going. And usually I don't. She knows I get lost in there as it is like a maze.

It was awful when we lost my mum. She had a stroke, which she recovered from, then another massive one not long after. She was 76. My dad didn't know what to do with himself. I would be the same if, God forbid, anything happened to Sandra. I wouldn't have a clue, I would be more than useless. Like my dear old dad, I wouldn't know how to work the washing machine or how to turn on the iron. He didn't know how to cook or use the oven, either. He would have fish and chips or pie and mash from the local shop every single day.

Despite not being at all domesticated, my dad was still independent. He would still take the train up to see Jamie play in Liverpool, and then up to north London when he was at

Spurs. Even though he was an Arsenal fan, it didn't bother him going to White Hart Lane – in fact, he loved it. He wouldn't miss a game and Jamie loved having him there.

My dad had an eye for a good player, too. I know I've said he would have made a good professional player, but he wouldn't have been a bad scout. I remember the time he watched West Ham youth team play Chelsea in west London and he told me about this fantastic young player he had seen. At the time, I was managing the first team, but my dad always had his eye out on the upcoming stars of the future.

I'd been up at Newcastle that day, so I'd missed the match, but my dad could not wait to tell me how they got on.

"I've seen the best kid I have seen in years today, Harry," he told me. "I know he is still in the youth squad, but I am telling you, you will want to keep an eye on him."

"Oh yeah," I said, intrigued. "What is this player's name? You are not talking about our Frank, are you, Dad?"

"No, his name is Ferdinand. He is a really tall lad, brilliant on the ball. He is a midfielder. I mean, what a player. No one could get near him."

"Rio?" I asked.

"That's the one. Rio Ferdinand," Dad said.

"Nah, he is still at school, Dad, he only started training with us a few weeks ago," I told him.

"I'm telling you Harry, he is one to watch," he said.

A few weeks later, Tony Carr, who was the youth team coach at the time, called me. We would often chat about the team, players who were doing well, who we wanted to progress, that sort of thing. The youth team ended up beating Chelsea in the final and Tony was obviously thrilled.

"What a game we had against Chelsea the other day," he told me.

"I know Tone, my dad was there and told me it was a great game. It is a shame I missed it."

"You need to get down to training one day Harry, you've got to come and see one of these young players. I threw him in and he was brilliant. Unbelievable."

"He sounds brilliant, maybe one to watch," I said. "What is his name?" I asked.

"Ferdinand," he said. "He is only 15, but he is absolutely fantastic and I can see a lot of potential."

"You're not the only one," I smiled.

I eventually signed Rio for West Ham in 1996 and never regretted it. He was so good, just like my dad said, that Millwall wanted him too, but Frank Sr talked him round. Rio was a south London boy and Millwall was his local club, so I could see the appeal for them to have a local boy on their books. But Frank Sr did a good job to get him to stay with us and he went on to have an absolutely fantastic career. Leeds broke the transfer record when they signed him for £18million in 2000 and then two years later in 2022, Manchester United broke the record again when they bought him for £30 million.

I told Rio the story about how my dad spotted him and I think my dad was quite pleased with himself.

Towards the end of my dad's life, I realised he couldn't live on his own any longer. One day he was on a bus going home, probably from a football match, when it suddenly jerked forwards and he flew out of his seat and smacked his head on the floor. He was checked out and all seemed okay, but it made me think.

Sandra and I had a chat about how he was coping on his own, and we decided together that he should come and live with us in Bournemouth. I hated the thought of him walking around on his own, or falling and no one finding him, so that was it, the decision was made, Dad was moving down to be with us. But then, some months later, he was diagnosed with brain cancer. I don't know if that fall on the bus brought the cancer on, they say it can do that, you know, if you have a cancer and then a fall can stir it up. And then within months he was gone. One thing that gives me great comfort is how proud my mum and dad were of Mark and Jamie. They got to see them grow up, start their families and, for my dad, he got to follow Jamie all over the country playing football. He definitely lived a good life.

Chapter 27

Struck down out of the blue

'The reality is, had I not gone to the hospital that day, I would have been in desperate trouble. Jane calling the ambulance and getting me there saved my life'

Sandra

"Sandra, you are not making any sense." My friend, Jane, had a look of concern on her face.

I had been out shopping and felt fine that morning. But all of a sudden, I started to get pains all over my body and felt very hot.

"I think we need to take you to the hospital," Jane said.

"What do you mean? I'm, I'm… fine. I'm… I will be okay in a minute, I am fine," I told her.

"Sandra, you are disorientated, you are not speaking properly," she said.

And then I gave in. I really wasn't feeling well and then all of a sudden, crash. I woke up in the ambulance. I looked around to a familiar scene – I have been in the back of one of these before. The paramedic was checking me over and Jane was sitting behind him, with a worried look on her face.

My body started to shake all over and I felt so cold, yet so hot. It was a sensation I had experienced the previous May when I had sepsis. Surely it was not happening again.

I had recently had a kidney infection and had been given antibiotics. I know that kidney infections can often make you feel disorientated if they are not cleared up by medication properly. Surely it must be that.

"We are taking you straight to A&E," the paramedic said. "We need you to be seen by a doctor urgently."

On the sirens went, the reflection of the blue lights flashing through the windows. Jane tried to get through to Harry, who was in London. "You need to make your way back," she told him.

I remember thinking it was a fuss over nothing, I didn't need to go to hospital. Harry doesn't need to come back from London – I will be okay in a little while.

But the reality is, had I not gone to the hospital that day, I would have been in desperate trouble. Jane calling the ambulance and getting me there saved my life. She saved my life.

Sepsis is such a horrible infection. It is life-threatening and can come on very quickly. It is basically blood poisoning, or what they used to call septicaemia many years ago, and starts from an infection in your body. It then starts to damage all the organs in your body – it is like your body is attacking itself – and that is why you have to act quickly, because it can take over your body in no time at all and you can go into septic shock.

I was very lucky that day. It took me a while to recover from it the second time around, so much so that when Harry was offered a huge opportunity, he was having second thoughts.

Chapter 28

Into the unknown

'I had never watched the show before, but how hard could it be? The grandkids were desperate for me to take part'

Harry

If there is one thing Sandra and I have learned in all our years together, it is that your health is the most important thing in the world. At the end of the day, wealth doesn't bring you happiness. You can have all the money in the world, but that won't help you. It is good health and being happy that is worth so much more. It's precious.

It is really scary when you love someone as much as I love Sandra, and you spend your whole life with them, and then they fall ill. You worry something is going to happen to them.

When Sandra had sepsis, it was bad. Very, very bad. But I couldn't think about losing her. I just couldn't. I wouldn't be able to handle it.

Looking back, it was a terrifying time. I still find it hard to think about now. She was so ill. If she hadn't got into the ambulance that night, she would have been in desperate trouble, so the quick-thinking of her friend, Jane, and the ambulance crew saved her. And we'll forever be grateful for that.

More people die from sepsis a year than the three major cancers. I didn't know that until I was invited by a charity to a lunch a year after Sandra had the deadly infection. I wanted to help raise awareness, but I also wanted to learn more about it. It was an emotional day. We heard the story of a young rugby player, very promising and a huge talent, and he got sepsis from a cut in his leg and died. He was only 19.

It is such a horrific infection, it takes over your whole body, and for those lucky enough to survive, it can take months to recover.

I had signed up to go into the *I'm a Celebrity* jungle. I had never watched the show before, but how hard could it be? The grandkids were desperate for me to take part and wouldn't stop going on about it.

"Harry, you do know you don't get very much food. It is all rice and beans," Sandra said.

"No, never," I said. "They can't do that to you, they have to feed you."

"Seriously Harry, it is rice and beans – and that is if you don't win a meal. When you do, it is wallabies and strange things like that," Sandra said.

"They might show that on TV, but there will be a van around the back somewhere," I told her. "There will be a place to get a bacon sandwich and a cup of tea. The rice and beans are all for show. They just want you to look hungry, but they have got to feed you some decent grub."

"I don't think it is Harry," she said.

I hold my hands up and say I had never seen an episode of *I'm a Celebrity*, not one single minute of it. The only things I watch on TV are the news, Sky Sports and the racing, and in the mornings I listen to TalkSport. But Sandra was a fan of the show and when I was offered the chance to go in, was quick to fill me in on how it all works.

"You have to do trials," she said. "You will have bugs and things thrown at you. In some trials, you have to eat them." Then she said, "Do you think this is a good idea Harry, you have never watched the show."

"How hard could it be?" I told her. "Plus the grandkids will love it, they want me to do it."

Days before I was due to fly to Australia, I nearly pulled out. Not because I got cold feet about staying in camp and eating rice and beans, but because Sandra wasn't 100 per cent and she needed the all clear from the doctor to fly. I didn't want to leave her.

"Harry, I am fine," she told me. "Molly is here to look after me and we are flying out a few days after you."

"I won't go Sarn," I told her. "If you are still not well the day before, I am scrubbing it. I am not going to go to Australia and do a show if you are not well."

But Sandra did get the all clear and I soon found myself at the airport waiting for a flight to Brisbane. I spent the time thinking about what we could do once we were over there. I was sure I would only be in the jungle for a few days. I told myself I would be one of the first to get voted out, then me and Sandra could have a bit of time relaxing in the sun and seeing the sights. That was the plan.

Never in a million years did I think I would be in there for nearly three weeks, let alone winning the show! I am a betting man and I wouldn't have bet on myself!

When I touched down at Brisbane airport, I was met by a New Zealander called Tina, and this great big fella, who I later found out was an ex-All Black rugby player.

"Mr Redknapp, welcome to Australia!" Tina said. "I will be your chaperone for the next six days and will look after you until you go into camp."

"Hi there," I said, scanning the burly rugby player.

"Mr Redknapp, you're now in lockdown. May I have your laptop and mobile phone, please?"

"Laptop? I don't own a laptop!" I told her.

"Okay, can you hand over your iPad tablet?" she asked.

"I don't have one of those either," I said. Tina obviously didn't realise I was a technophobe and can just about work my mobile phone.

"We are going to need that too," she said.

"Okay, but I just need to give my wife a call back home," I said, scrolling through my phone book.

"That won't be possible, I am afraid," Tina said. "We need to put you on lockdown."

"I have to tell Sandra I have arrived," I pleaded. "She will be worried sick. She isn't going to know what has happened to me."

In the end, Tina let me make the call. If she hadn't, I would have been on the first plane out of there. I got through to Sandra straight away.

We then made our way out of the airport and to the car. The rugby player fella drove us for about an hour and a half. No one told me where we were going, only that me and the other campmates would be staying in separate hotels until the show started. I say hotel... when we pulled up it was a rundown motel with an old-looking pool that I didn't fancy swimming in. I thought we would be staying in Versace for a few nights before we went in, a bit of luxury before we went to camp, but no. Then I got my room number. Tina was staying next door.

"Let me know if you need anything or want to go for a walk, Harry," Tina said. "I can't let you out of my sight, so just give me a shout."

After a couple of days, I was becoming a bit claustrophobic. Tina, as lovely as she was, was like my shadow, and I was struggling to eat anything at the hotel as the food was diabolical.

I looked at the clock. It was 6am. Right, I thought, I am going to go out and have a cup of coffee by myself. I got myself dressed, opened the door, and very slowly and quietly made my way down to the hotel reception. With my coffee, I pulled up a chair by the pool, sat down and closed my eyes. Peace. I thought.

"Morning Harry!" came a familiar voice. I jumped out of my skin.

"Morning Tina," I said.

"Harry, I have told you, you can't just sneak off without me," she said.

"Oh give me a break, Tina," I said. "I am only having a cup of coffee."

"I have never had a winner, you know," she said, changing the subject, probably sensing I wasn't in the mood to talk.

"What do you mean?"

"A winner of the show. In all my years doing this show, it has been 10 years now, and I have never been the chaperone of the winner."

"Well, sorry Tina, but you won't have any luck this year," I told her. "Listen, can we go out for dinner tonight? I can't stand the food here and I need to get out."

"Of course," she smiled. "No problem."

Later that night we headed to the marina. Tina said I needed shorts for swimming in camp and I hadn't packed any, so we popped into the shops before finding a nice Italian restaurant.

"This is more like it," I told her, as we were shown to our seats. The owner approached us with his order pad.

"Mr Redknapp!" he said. "Welcome, welcome!" He told me he was Croatian and I have had a lot of Croatian players play for me over the years. "You had Modric at Tottenham," he said.

"Can I get you a drink, maybe a nice bottle of wine?" he asked.

"Yes I will have wine, please," I said.

"And your wife?" he said with a smile.

"No, no, she isn't my wife," I said.

"No problem Mr Redknapp," he said, winking at me. "I understand."

"No, no, no, you don't understand!" I told him. "She isn't my wife, she is my..." What could I say? I was sworn to secrecy, so I couldn't tell him she was my chaperone and that I was going into the jungle. "Never mind," I said.

The next morning it was time to pack up and leave. I got into the car with Tina so we could make our way to the camp.

"Right, Harry, I need to blindfold you," she said.

"You what? What for?" I asked her.

"Sorry Harry, that is what happens. We can't show you where you are going," she said.

So I sat there, for another hour and a half car journey with a blindfold on. It was very strange.

"We are here," Tina said. I got out of the car and the first thing I saw was a little tent type thing with a few plastic chairs outside. We must have been there for an hour before a guide came along.

"Okay Harry, back in the car we go," Tina said.

"What do you mean? Where are we going?" I asked.

"To camp, this was a pit stop. I need to put your blindfold back on," she said.

So with a sense of déjà vu, I was back in the car, blindfolded and not knowing where I was going.

Eventually we arrived at a hilltop. "This is you, Harry," Tina said. "Make your way over there and your campmates will meet you. I'll see you on the other side. Good luck – and I hope you win!"

I was waiting on the hilltop, it was grey and cold and I started to wish I had worn a jacket over my shirt. It was there I met former *X Factor* singer Fleur East, Anne Hegerty, from *The Chase*, and Nick Knowles, Britain's famous DIY handyman. We were whisked away in a helicopter and then the first trial began. It was called Hell Holes and required us to drive around, putting our hands in holes which had God knows what in them. First we had to pick a driver.

"I used to think I was a good driver, but I had a nightmare and ran over my wife one day," I told them. Into the passenger seat I went.

Next up was a boat race – we hadn't even got into camp yet and we were already doing trials, but this one was important. Whoever won would get the best camp. There was no comparison – the teams were a complete mismatch. We had John Barrowman who was as fit as a fiddle, and Nick who looked strong, but I could also tell was competitive. Completing our team were a couple of youngsters, Sair Khan and Malique Thompson–Dwyer. We were sure to win, and we did. But as I got out of the water to celebrate with my team-mates, I twisted my knee. It was so painful and not what I needed on the first day. And to make matters worse, later that night I felt the flu coming on. I think being in that cold swamp made me feel ill, and sleeping under a tarpaulin sheet didn't help. 'I hope they don't tell Sandra I feel like this,' I thought, 'she will be worried sick and want me out of there!'

Chapter 29

A surreal experience

'I thought he would only last a few days, he would be one of the first voted out. I should have had a bit more faith in him'

Sandra

Watching Harry on the TV was a bit surreal. Of course, I have seen him on TV many times over the years, giving post-match interviews and commentary. But seeing him on *I'm a Celebrity* was different because Harry didn't know what he was letting himself in for. Being interviewed after a game is easy for Harry, he lives and breathes football and could talk about it all day. He is comfortable. But going into the Australian jungle with a bunch of strangers, not being able to call me or the boys and not being able to have his morning coffee, I just thought he is not going to like it at all.

When Harry Met Sandra

I had warned Harry about the food and the small portions before he went in. He didn't believe me, and thought there was a caravan out back serving up sandwiches and hot drinks all day. I think he still believed that until the first night he was in there.

Despite that, I knew Harry would be okay with the lack of food – he has never been a big eater and often doesn't have lunch. He would quite happily go without. But I did worry about the trials and what he might have to do. It is one thing not eating, but eating animal parts is something else! And while Harry is an early riser, he loves his home comforts, and I couldn't imagine he would enjoy sleeping in a hammock or on a damp floor. And not only that, but Harry is in his 70s; he is no spring chicken any more – neither of us are! – and so I was worried about how he would cope.

I was due to fly to Australia with our granddaughter Molly in a week's time. Friends and family were invited to join the crew out there once the voting had started. I was excited to go. I hadn't been to Australia before – Harry had for a football work trip when he was managing Jordan for a while, but I hadn't been.

"We can have a nice holiday together once I am out of the jungle," Harry said. "I'll be voted out after a few days and then we can spend the rest of the time seeing the sights and relaxing."

A surreal experience

It sounded ideal. Molly and I were also told we would be staying at the five-star Versace hotel while we waited for Harry to be voted out. I had seen previous contestants return to the Versace after their stint in camp and it looked lovely. The celebrities are usually interviewed on breakfast television by the pool the next morning after leaving camp, and it always looked so calm and relaxing.

I was starting to feel better after having sepsis. It took months to properly recover, but I was deemed fit to fly.

"I am not going if you are still unwell," Harry told me a few days before he was due to fly out. "I'll sack it off now."

"Don't be silly, I am fine!" I told him. "I am with Molly and if, God forbid, anything happened, they would let you know. But it won't – it will all be fine."

Molly and I made our way to Heathrow and boarded the flight to Sydney. I couldn't wait to see Harry.

In all our years of marriage we have never been apart for a long time, and whenever Harry was away with work, he would always call. It was the longest time I had ever gone without speaking to him. The last phone call was when Harry touched down in Sydney and told me his phone was being taken away. I now couldn't speak to him until he came out of the jungle.

I thought he would only last a few days, he would be one of the first voted out. I should have had a bit more faith in him really, because as time went on, and as I watched Harry during the trials and as his friendships with the other camp-mates grew, I thought to myself, he could actually go and win this.

Chapter 30

Out of the jungle and into the limelight

'Sandra has been my rock throughout our marriage. She has been there to pick up the pieces when I have felt broken. Now, the rest of the country can see what an amazing and special woman she is'

Harry

"It is okay Harry, you and me are okay," Noel Edmonds whispered in my ear. Declan Donnelly and Holly Willoughby, who was drafted in to replace Dec's sidekick Ant McPartlin as host that year, were both standing in front of us holding cards. It was the first public vote and one of us was going home.

"This doesn't concern me or you," Noel went on. "We won't be going anywhere."

While I thought I would be voted out of the camp in the first few days, I'll admit I didn't want to be first. After that, I didn't mind what happened. I guess it is that competitive streak in me – going first meant I was the loser, and I didn't want to be first out.

"Rita, it could be you," Dec and Holly said, followed by "Noel, it could be you."

I could feel the disappointment coming off Noel and he looked worried.

"The first person to be voted out of the *I'm a Celebrity* jungle is…"

This is horrible, I thought. I am not in the bottom two but I could feel the tension. My heart was racing and my mouth was dry, I felt like it was a penalty shoot-out. Who was it going to be?

"It's Noel."

The first night in the jungle, Emily Atack explained to me how the public vote worked.

"How many days till the first one goes?" I asked her.

"10 days," she said.

"10 days? I thought someone would be going tomorrow."

She laughed. She thought I was joking. "Seriously Emily, the first person goes in 10 days?" I said. "Yes Harry! Did you not watch the show?" she laughed again.

Noel took his fate on the chin, but I could see he was disappointed. He also didn't think he was going home a few minutes earlier, so he was probably shocked too. As we made our way over to the bridge, Noel said he was looking forward to being reunited with his wife Liz, who was a clairvoyant.

"I wonder if she saw that coming," I joked, as Noel walked over the bridge and we made our way back to camp.

Noel was a really nice fella. They all were and I am lucky to say I got on with everyone. I know that doesn't always happen on these shows, but they were so lovely.

James McVey, from The Vamps, was a really nice guy. He was a third of my age, so I guess I was a bit like a father figure to him. He would ask me a lot of questions about Sandra, our marriage and what made it work. He also asked me lots of questions about how I proposed, so I wasn't at all surprised when, about six weeks after leaving camp, James popped the question to his long-term partner Kirstie Brittain. In fact, Sandra and I attended their wedding at Lulworth Castle in Dorset in October 2021. They would have got married sooner, but they had to keep postponing it due to the pandemic. But it was worth the wait for them – it was a stunning wedding and a beautiful sunny day.

James and I still stay in touch. We had a WhatsApp group with everyone on it, but it is fading out a bit now. I don't go on it very often, but then I am not great with all these groups and whatnot.

It was a great experience, but there were low moments for us all in the jungle. I am not one for big meals, which was lucky really as the food was diabolical. There were a few days when I just couldn't eat. I couldn't face it. One day we were given something like a wallaby foot or something weird like that, and it put me off. Sandra warned me the food was very strange and nothing was normal. Even the rice tasted awful. It was a surprise that I had only lost a stone when I came out!

For me, the best parts were when you didn't have to do a trial. Camp was so quiet when others were out doing tasks and I would use that time to go and crash out on a hammock and have a kip for an hour or so. But they were very long days – I would be up at 5am and we were going to bed so late at night. I was on full-time dunny duty, which the rest of the campmates were pleased about. I was given the role after telling them how I had lost my sense of smell in the 1990 crash and that it hadn't ever come back. I couldn't cook and didn't know how to wash up, so I felt clearing out the dunny was the least I could do.

As the days slowly went by and my campmates were going one by one – Malique, Sair, Rita Simons, Anne Hegerty – I started to wonder what was going on? I couldn't believe no one was voting me out. A bit of dread washed over me – I could be here till the end. I didn't go in it to win it. But there were people in there who I could tell wanted to win. Nick was competitive and I could tell John wanted to win. He'd watched all the series and hinted at as much.

Then Nick was gone, then James – not James, I thought, I was sure he was going to win it – then Fleur. What a lovely girl she was.

And then there were three – me, John and Emily. The next day, we all had our final challenge, each tasked with winning a dish for our final meal in camp. Mine was called Danger Down Under, where I had to be strapped underground while cockroaches and crickets crawled all over me. Then in came the rats – I hadn't told anyone I was terrified of the things. I kept thinking of my family – Sandra worrying about me, and Mark and Jamie cracking up laughing to see me suffer.

And then came the final vote. John came third and it was between me and Emily. I thought Emily had won it. She was a good girl with a heart of gold. She was very funny and kept our spirits up most days. She told me she had a soft spot for Jamie too and wanted me to set him up with her when we left. She was funny.

Emily and I made our way out of the camp for the final time where we went to meet Dec and Holly for our interviews. As they showed me my highlights, I couldn't believe I was sitting there. I have not made many finals in my career. I was also five minutes from seeing Sandra. I couldn't wait to see her again. I wanted them to hurry up.

"The 2018... King of the Jungle is Harry!"

What? No! This can't be happening. This can't be right. What is going on? They must have got it wrong. I honestly couldn't believe it. Who the bloody hell was voting for me?

The reunion with Sandra on the bridge was pretty special. Fireworks were going off and photographers were calling us towards them. I suddenly realised Sandra had become a bit of a celebrity overnight, though I knew she would absolutely hate that. She has always wanted a quiet life. "Sandra, turn this way, Sandra, move in closer to Harry," they shouted as the cannons went off.

Before long, we were making our way back to the Palazzo Versace. It wasn't as glamorous and high end as I thought. I thought it was going to be five-star pure luxury, that is certainly what I had been led to believe as my fellow campmates were raving about it and said how they couldn't wait to stay there. But the hotel looked quite tired and the corridors had plates of half-eaten food outside some rooms. It was very disappointing. That said, I couldn't wait for a shower, a cup of coffee and a decent meal. I was also absolutely shattered and couldn't wait to get into bed, but first was an interview with Piers Morgan and Kate Garraway on GMB and then a party with everyone in camp and their families.

"I don't even know what I have done, Kate," I told her during my poolside interview. "It is not like winning a football match. It was not easy at all, it was hard. It was tough physically and it was a completely new world for me. Some of the days were long and hard. Sleeping was horrendous, but everyone in there was great, I couldn't say one bad word about them. It was absolutely fantastic."

Out of the jungle and into the limelight

Piers – a great man who I have known for many years through football and who is a constant wind-up as he is one of those annoyingly smug Arsenal fans – then asked what the secret of mine and Sandra's marriage was. It is a question I often get embarrassed about because for us there is no secret, we just love being together.

"Me and Sandra were just 17 when we met and we've never been apart," I told him. "I don't care what people think – I love her like mad. She is my life. Jamie always says, 'Dad, how did you pull her? You have punched so high above your weight it is unbelievable,' and he is not wrong."

The next day, they were throwing us out of the hotel. I didn't even have a proper kip. We were all only booked in until the day after the final, so when the next morning came, it was time to clear us out.

Sandra and I had decided to stop off in Dubai on our way back and have a holiday, just the two of us. We had planned to stay in the same hotel that we always stay in, and we were looking forward to relaxing and having a quiet break.

On our first night, we booked into a steak restaurant that we love. It seats around 200 people and is a popular place for tourists.

We both walked in and waited to be seated, thinking about the delicious food and wine we were going to have. All of a sudden, a bloke shouts out across the restaurant, "There's only one Harry Redknapp!" All the other diners turn, put their knives and forks down and stand up to join in. "There's only one Harry Redknapp," they all sang.

"I thought we were going to have a quiet holiday," Sandra said as I smiled.

We got to the table and I called Jamie.

"It is all going off here Jim Bob, it's mad, me and your mum have come out for a bit of dinner, and they are all singing to me. What on earth is going on?" I told him.

"Wait till you get home, Dad," he told me. "Your face is everywhere, everyone is talking about you and mum, it is just incredible."

It was funny, really, as Jamie was one person who didn't want me to go into the jungle. "Dad, this is a big mistake, don't do it," he said. But now he will say it is one of the best things I did.

And that was the start of it, really. It was a whole new world to me. I am used to going on TalkSport or Sky Sports and talking about football, but now everyone is asking me about me and Sandra. "Tell us about that night at the Two Puddings? Was it love at first sight?"

The next day on the beach, we had people coming up to us for selfies. Sandra and I like to sit in a quiet spot, away from everyone else, but people found us and were coming up for a chat, asking Sandra for pictures. It was all mad.

Out of the jungle and into the limelight

Sandra has been my rock throughout our marriage. She is an absolutely fantastic mother and grandmother, she has been there to pick up the pieces when I have felt broken, she has put up with me when I have been dreadful company, she knows what to say at the right time, and she has been there for me at my lowest – losing Bobby, losing Brian, the trial. Now, the rest of the country can see what an amazing and special woman she is.

Chapter 31

Our family gets bigger

'Now we had a new baby in the family – another boy! – little Rafa, and I couldn't wait to meet him'

Sandra

"He is here, Mum!" Jamie had called me to give me the happy news. Our eighth grandchild had arrived, and they had named him Rafael, or Rafa, for short.

"Send me some pictures when you can, darling," I said to him. "Is Frida doing okay?"

"We're all good, Mum," he said. I'll call you later."

It is not unusual for Jamie to call me every day, but that call was extra special. Even though Jamie doesn't live nearby, he is always on the phone, checking I am okay. I have been used to Jamie living far away from me ever since he went to Liverpool at the age of 17. He was up there for 11 years before he moved down to London to join Tottenham, still many miles away from Bournemouth. Jamie has always been quite independent, and he was always so determined to be a good player, that he was happy anywhere where he could play. He is like Harry in that respect. Harry travelled around a lot as a footballer and a manager. He was never away for long periods of time, but being a football manager meant he was up and down the country every weekend. Even now Harry and Jamie are here, there and everywhere, and are always on the go. They are so busy. Harry is meant to be winding down, but he can't help himself. It is like as soon as he has a gap in his diary, it needs to be filled with something. And if it isn't for work, he is on the golf course or at the races. Mark is more like me and is more of a homebody. He has lived down in Bournemouth since we moved here in 1976 and, apart from when we lived in America, he hasn't lived anywhere else. Bournemouth is his home, and he loves it down here. I feel lucky that I have some of my grandkids living so close to me, and I see Molly most days. But it is hard being far away from Jamie and his boys, and we don't see them as much as I would like as they are in London.

Now we had a new baby in the family – another boy! – little Rafa, and I couldn't wait to meet him. My phone pinged

– Jamie had sent over some pictures. One of him holding Rafa in hospital and one of little Rafa on his own – he had quite a mop of hair, a bit like Mark and Jamie did.

Jamie and Frida had been together for just over a year when Rafa was born. They had met the summer before and when Jamie introduced us to her, we thought she was lovely.

Like Jamie, she had been married before and has a girl and three boys with her ex-husband. And just like Jamie is with his two sons, Frida's ex is very much involved in raising their kids, and I think that is so important.

When Frida was pregnant with Rafa, Jamie proposed. No one apart from family and close friends knew they were even engaged until they got married at a registry office in November 2021. Jamie isn't into the showbiz world, and that didn't change when he met Frida, so announcing his news just isn't something he would ever have done.

As we arrived at Chelsea Old Town Hall, I could see there were some photographers waiting.

Harry and I – I was wearing a floral print dress, Harry in a smart blue suit and tie – went up to the hall door. Harry started banging. Nothing. So he banged again. Then two people passing by told us we were at the wrong door and pointed us in the right direction. Harry looked over at the photographers and gave a shrug and a smile, but I was so embarrassed. I just wanted to get in there.

Our family gets bigger

Jamie and Frida's wedding was a small ceremony with just 30 close family and friends including Charley and Beau, Mark and Lucy, and Frank and Christine. Frida looked absolutely beautiful. Her dress was stunning. It was an off-the-shoulder dress and her bump looked all nice and neat. It was a classic dress and suited her perfectly. And Jamie looked handsome in his navy suit and tie. After the service, we all went to Scott's restaurant in Mayfair for dinner in a private dining room. It was relaxed and everyone really enjoyed themselves. I remember thinking about how happy they looked when Jamie and Frida cut their cake. There was a smile between them. It is lovely to see Jamie happy, it is all Harry and I can ask for.

All we want is for our boys to be happy. That is all we have ever wanted.

Chapter 32

Sixty years together

'I've been the football manager, but behind the scenes, it is Sandra who is managing me. I don't know what I would do without her'

Harry

In a couple of years, Sandra and I will have been together for 60 years. Sixty years since we first met on the dance floor on the Two Puddings. Sixty years of putting up with me! People always ask what the secret to our marriage is and I don't know how to answer that really, I don't think there is one. I love Sandra, and I'm lucky enough that she loves me. We are just a normal couple and we don't think there is anything special about us, really. Sandra doesn't like it that people think we are this amazing couple who can survive anything, because there are marriages that don't survive, and there is nothing wrong in that. I guess we are just lucky. Well, I am very lucky.

I know I haven't been easy to live with over the years. There have been times when I've got lost in the job and brought the stress of it home with me, and that hasn't been fair on Sandra. I know I haven't always been the easiest person to live with. There have been times when I have come home from a loss and been in a terrible mood, and that can't have been nice for her. There are some wives who wouldn't have stood for it, but Sandra has just always been so reassuring, and that's why she is the only person who could make me feel better when I had those low points during my career. I've been the football manager, but behind the scenes, it is Sandra who is managing me. I don't know what I would do without her. She means everything to me.

Sandra
'I don't know what I would do without Mr Pastry'

I know I always joke about Harry being like 'Mr Pastry' and how he has got me into several messes over the years, but I really don't know what I would do without him. He has always looked after us as a family and everything he has ever done, it's been for us, his family. He gets under my feet when he is at home, but I miss him when he isn't around. He is my best friend. We love being together and my favourite thing to do is go for a nice meal with Harry at our local Italian restaurant or our 9am coffee on a Saturday morning at the local café. We are quite a simple couple, really. I'm not one for the limelight, and neither is Harry, really. He might appear on TV, but when he is at home, he likes the quieter life. Things really changed for Harry when he went into the jungle and he is probably busier now than he has ever been, and definitely the least stressed!

It's quite scary that almost 60 years have passed. In some ways it feels like yesterday, and in others I look back and think about how much we've been lucky enough to do, the wonderful places we have visited. We've had such a wonderful time together. I really wouldn't change a thing, even the bad bits, because as I always say, what doesn't kill you makes you stronger.

Epilogue

Our Harry and Sandra

Mark Redknapp, son

My memories of growing up with Mum and Dad are great. We grew up down in Bournemouth and moved there when I was three, and at that time we didn't have a lot of money. Dad was playing for Bournemouth, but in the meantime he was selling cars out of the local newspapers. Every Friday the local paper would come out, and it was time to sell the cars. He would do it with his mate, Colin, in London.

I remember one day someone came to buy a car and it wouldn't start, but my dad was away. I remember my mum

223

was heavily pregnant with Jamie at the time and I was a toddler, but my mum is pushing this car up the road to get it to start with the geezer in it! All of a sudden, a little rabbit escaped from our back garden and started running up the road. So my mum goes from pushing the car, to running after this rabbit, and pushing the car. It was mad. She sold it though! And she made about £15 out of it. But that is all dad would make, £15 or £20 out of selling cars, but it meant that they could give us the best life. It is amazing how they did that.

My mum and dad would both always make sure we had everything we wanted, and my dad wouldn't see us go without, he is that sort of person. Me and Jamie always had presents at Christmas and it was always made special for us.

We never used to go on holidays abroad when we were younger. Instead, we would always go to Leysdown where my nan and grandad, Violet and Harry, had a caravan and me and Jamie would spend the whole of the six weeks holidays down there. It was the best time of our lives, really.

We also had some great times when we moved to America in 1977. I have some brilliant memories from our time out there. We were over there for six months of the year, and went to school there, and then we would be back in England for six months, and then we would go to school here. It was brilliant. We had the best of both worlds.

Our Harry and Sandra

Then, in 1980 we moved to Phoenix and we were looking to stay out there for good, so my mum and dad decided to rent our house out in England. But when Dad's cheques started bouncing after about two months and he wasn't getting any wages; that is when he realised his job had all been a con. So we had to come back to England with no money and nowhere to live. It was a very hard time for my mum and dad, not that they would ever let me and Jamie know that.

We ended up renting a council house from Dad's mate, Mad Mick. But even then when they had nothing, we still had the best time because my mum and dad always made sure me and Jamie had everything. One of the things I remember growing up was how much my mum and dad cared about us having manners. We were always taught to say please and thank you. I've had some ups and downs myself over the years, but I have always had good morals and good manners. They instilled that in me and Jamie as young kids. and I've done the same with my children. My children have amazing manners, and people are always surprised by how incredibly polite they are. That all comes down from what I learnt from my mum and dad.

Me and my dad are very close. We work together and run a property development business called Pierfront Developments. He gives me carte blanche to buy properties, and as long as I return the right money on them and make a profit, he is happy. If I don't, he will probably give me the sack! We have a really good business relationship and have meetings every morning. There isn't a day that goes by that I don't speak to him. It is not all about work though, I can chat to my dad about anything.

My dad was quite tough on us when we were younger. When I was a teenager I used to play for my dad with Jamie for Bournemouth reserves and I used to have a lot of injuries. I remember one day I came off the pitch and I knew I had done my ankle. I was like, "Oh God, this is so painful." I went for an X-ray and nothing showed up. It was still hurting me, so I went for another X-ray and still nothing showed up. I carried on playing, but I remember playing in tears because it was hurting me so much. I think my dad probably thought I was a big baby, and maybe I was being a big baby, but he carried on pushing me to play. But what we didn't know was that I had actually chipped three bones in my ankle. Obviously, my dad didn't know this, but I know he pushed me to be better – and I could probably have been a bit better! – and to carry on because he wanted the best for me. He was always on me and always on Jamie, and that has made us the people we are today. We are driven.

I look up to my dad like he is a king. I know everyone will say that about their own dad, but I think our dad is an incredible man. And everyone thinks it; everywhere he goes he has people telling him how much they love him. When I go out with him, I don't get to talk to him as he has so many people coming up to him wanting to meet him. I think when he went into the jungle, he opened himself up to a whole new genre of people – you didn't just have the people who knew him as a footballer and a manager, but he now had people who loved him who were maybe not into football.

Even my mum has become a bit of a celebrity now, though she will hate me saying that! My mum is so laid back and she is a very kind person. She is always positive and is the sweetest person you can ever imagine. Again, I know everyone will say that about their own mum, but she is just amazing. Jamie and I have been very lucky that we both have such loving parents.

My mum and dad have the most amazing relationship. They just have something very special. There isn't any secret to their marriage and I can't put my finger on it, but they have something unique. They will go out for dinner two or three times a week and just be together. They haven't got a lot of friends – they have a lot of acquaintances – but they just love being in each other's company. Even when we were younger, I don't remember my dad being out with his mates, and I don't remember my mum having girls' nights out. They just always wanted to be together. There are not many people who can do that, spending all that time together and being around each other all of the time. But when you can, you know it is right. It is just incredible what they have got, really.

When me and Jamie both went on to get married, they guided us. They taught us that nothing can ever be perfect in life, and there are always ups and downs in any marriage. And my mum always says, never go to bed on an argument, which is funny as I don't think I have ever seen my mum and dad have an argument!

I just want to say to my mum and dad, I am so lucky that I have got you. If I have done things wrong in the past, you have always been there for me. There have been a couple of times when I have let you down, but you have both been amazing. You are fantastic, kind-hearted people, and I am blessed to have you as my mum and dad.

Jamie Redknapp, son

My mum and dad have got something very special. If you ask me what it is, I couldn't tell you. It really is impossible to put it down to one thing. There is just something unique about their relationship and about them as individuals. They're not busy-bodies. They don't try to take the limelight. They have never wanted anything apart from their two boys to be successful, but always with so much love.

Mark and I had a great upbringing. When you are a parent there is a love like no other, no one will care more about you than your mum and dad – I know that now as a dad myself – and me and Mark always felt that love, and still do now. They've always been amazing. They have never been embarrassing parents and they have never really got a lot wrong, and they will always give it to us straight when they have to.

I still speak to my mum every day. She has been the voice of reason for me throughout my life, and I always run everything by her. That makes me sound like a mummy's boy, but I'm not. My mum is the kindest person I have ever met. I can honestly say I have never heard her slag anyone off, ever. She hasn't got a bad word to say about anyone, and I don't know many people like that. I think it is the way she was brought up by her own mum and dad and the values they gave to her. And I love that about her so much because in the modern world that is pretty special. She really is a one-off.

My mum is my best mate and I always want to speak to her and make sure she is alright. She adores us and just cares for us all so deeply. She has such a kind heart. We just get on so well and I have a pure love for her, it is the only way I can explain it. Mark is the same, his relationship with my mum is just as close, different in some ways, but they adore each other too.

I wasn't really one of those kids that liked to go out growing up, and probably weirdly, I just wanted to be at home with my mum. She was a great cook and me and Mark would love to be in the garden playing football while we waited for our dinner. She just looked after us so well.

My mum is also a very nurturing nan. She loves all of her grandchildren. She loves coming up to see Rafa and when they are together, it is just adorable. It is a new thing for both of us; it has been 13 years since my last son, Beau, was born. Now I have gone full circle and I'm doing it again, and my mum is the same in that she gets a new baby grandchild again. When she holds Rafa, it makes me feel so happy. It really is so lovely to see. Everyone tells me that Rafa looks like my dad – unfortunately! – but I think my dad looks like every baby, haha!

My dad was always very supportive of me and Mark growing up, and he always came to watch us play. He took me to every single training session that he could. Both mum and dad would be at every event, just to be there for us and show their support.

Sport was always a massive part of our life, so education was secondary, which isn't always ideal. But I think I probably learned more that way. I probably got a Masters in people, learning how to deal with different situations, knowing how to be able to meet anybody from any background, and to be nice and show respect. Manners were one of the most important things to my mum and dad. Actually probably *the* most important. As a kid, if I ever forgot to say please or thank you or if I embarrassed them in any way in front of someone, they would not be happy. And that is so important to me now as an adult. It is the easiest thing in the world to have good manners, to say please and thank you, to look people in the eye when you're talking to them. They are the basic values that my mum and dad taught me and Mark. And now it is natural for me to be like that as a dad. If my boys were ever rude or bad mannered or spoke badly, well, I just can't have that.

I am probably a little tougher on my two elder boys' education than my mum and dad were on me and my brother. But there are two schools of thoughts on that − I went on to play for England and in my dad's own way he did something very special with me. My dad had a real influence on me, he saw something in me and pushed it, and I would say it was my mum who gave me my work ethic. She is very driven. And both my mum and dad have addictive personalities and I would say I am the same, I've got that from them.

My mum and dad also taught us that we have to work hard for everything because there are no shortcuts in life. I had always wanted to be successful in football and my mum and dad taught me that if you want to do something, you don't do it half-heartedly, you go and give it everything you have got.

I would say my mum has always been the sensible one out of the two of them because my dad is quite loose. He is the greatest guy, but he can sometimes be all over the place. He always has stuff going on in his head, and I am genuinely in awe of him sometimes because I couldn't do what he does. I've got the utmost respect for him because there is one thing I have never wanted to do, and that is to follow him into football management. I have seen the ups and downs of it all, and to be honest, the downs put me off. There were times during my dad's managing career when he would come home, and I'd look at him and I would just think, 'Why are you doing this, Dad?'

Even back in the early days when he wasn't earning any money from the game and we were struggling, he carried on, and he did it for us because he wanted me, my mum and Mark to be okay. He set us a great example.

I remember how my dad made me have a paper round to earn my own money. I was called the spare boy because I was a bit younger – if anyone didn't turn up, if they were ill, I would do the paper round on my BMX bike. But sometimes my dad would come with me, and we would go do it in the car. He would even jump out and post a few newspapers, and they couldn't believe it when Harry Redknapp started turning up at their door at 7 o'clock in the morning to deliver their newspapers! But I got my £3.70 every week. I think sometimes people think we were born with a silver spoon in our mouths, but it was anything but that. Don't get me wrong, there were people who were a lot worse off than we were, but we really didn't have money like people might think.

To see my dad work as hard as he did, it made me want to be like that, it made me want to achieve too. I wanted to follow in my dad's footsteps. Okay, I might have been a better footballer, but I wouldn't have been a better manager, that's for sure. I couldn't have competed; there is no way I could have got to 1,300 games as a manager like he did.

It is crazy the amount of people who say to me "your dad is the funniest guy I've ever met" and I think he could have been an actor or a comedian, but then I guess when you are a football manager you are almost an actor because you are up there and you have to pretend everything is okay.

I have a very close relationship with my dad. When I was younger, I used to go everywhere with him. I would bunk off school so I could go and train with him.

Don't get me wrong, my dad was strict at times. He was an amazing dad, but he could lose it if we didn't behave. We were always careful after he had lost a game, as he took his job very seriously and did not like losing. I remember when he would come home after a football match when he had lost, and he would be in a bad mood. Some people might say, "Okay you have lost, get on with it" but my mum was always so lovely and supportive. She would be like "Listen boys, don't say anything silly, I don't want your dad to be upset, go and watch a film" and then she would let him sulk and moan. And that was her way of handling it because she cared for him so much.

But if I am honest, and my dad knows this, that is why I don't like him watching the boys play too much because he is quite harsh on them. I say to him, "Just come as a grandad and enjoy it Dad," but I think it stresses him out because he gets uptight and wants to get involved. He just can't help it, it is in his nature to take sport so seriously. He won't suffer people who are not trying hard or giving it their all. That is what he finds the hardest. But it only comes from a good place because he wants them to do so well. When he looks at all of his grandkids, he just wants the best for them. He wants the best for all of us, especially my mum.

My dad genuinely loves my mum. He isn't a romantic – I can't ever remember him buying her flowers or making any romantic gestures – but he has this love for my mum that is worth more than anyone could ever buy as a gift. Some women need a man to buy them flowers every week of the year or send them gifts, but my dad didn't do that. He doesn't do that. He just adores her with every part of his body. My dad shows his love for my mum in a different way. He loves and protects her in his own way. His love is an affection of pure adulation. I guess he has always known how lucky he is, and I really respect him for that. I have always said he won the lottery by marrying Mum.

She is just so special, and is quite shy in a way. She has never wanted any sort of limelight, but I guess when my dad went into the jungle, that put them into another world. But I honestly think it has been the best thing that could happen to them. I think my dad has thrived after it, and it has really helped my mum because I think that she has enjoyed parts of it. I wouldn't say she is the sort of person that loves it all, like I say, she isn't one for the limelight, but it has been really nice for them both to have a new lease of life, and my dad is the calmest I have known him to be. It is incredible, really.

Our Harry and Sandra

I'm just so pleased he didn't listen to me because if he did, he wouldn't have done it. I really thought he was making the biggest mistake of his life, but I think he came across brilliantly. I think when people saw my mum and dad together, when they heard the way he spoke so highly of her, and when they saw how real they are together, they just fell in love with them as a couple.

That is why me and Mark are so lucky to call them mum and dad. I find it heartbreaking when people don't have a relationship with their mum, as we have been so fortunate and enriched to have the relationship we have with ours. I moved away from home at 17 to go to Liverpool, and I never really moved back to Bournemouth; I live in London now. It means I don't get to see my mum and dad as much as I would like to, but that doesn't stop me thinking about them or missing them.

It is hard to say what makes my relationship with my mum and dad so special. I just think they are a really great team. They work so well together. Because don't get me wrong, my dad hasn't always been easy to put up with, I don't think he will mind me saying that! He sometimes wants things his way, and my mum will go along with it, she is a real softie and is so gentle. She is always there for him and will support him whatever.

I know that dynamic might not work for everybody, with one person always having their way, but it works for them. I guess it has been about having a bit of give and take with both of them, and I think that is how it has to be with relationships.

Luckily, it works for my mum and dad and has done for all these years. They are truly inspiring to us all.

To Mum and Dad, thank you for all you have done for me, we are so lucky to have you. You are amazing and have made me the person I am today.

Molly Redknapp, granddaughter

To my grandparents and my best friends, there are not enough words to describe how thankful I am for you both. For every lesson, for all your unconditional love, Pops for every story and Nan for teaching us all how to always be kind and calm, oh and for making the best Tottenham cake! They say a grandparent's love feels like nobody else's and this couldn't be more true. You both have always been one phone call away and give the best guidance and support.

Thank you both for always being the best x

Love Molly x x

Bobbie Redknapp, grandson

My Pop is a very good person to talk to about football. He knows everything you need to have to become a footballer.

He changed my position in football for me to become the best player I can be. My nanny really can do anything. They both mean the world to all the family.

They both look after everyone and are the nicest people you will ever meet and always inspire us to do anything.

Frank Lampard, nephew

I have very fond memories of Harry and Sandra growing up. We are a close family, and even though Harry and Sandra lived down in Bournemouth, and we were in Essex, there was still that close connection. Especially for my mum, Pat, and Sandra. They were very close and I remember them being on the phone constantly. It was very normal for me growing up and hearing my mum chatting to Auntie Sandra. I think they relied on each other a lot. They would plan trips for us to go down and see Harry and Sandra in Bournemouth in the summer holidays. I loved it as they had a big beautiful house and a lovely garden. Sandra was always so welcoming. I got to have a kick about with Jamie and Mark and it was lovely – it felt nice to be away from the Essex suburbs. My dad and Harry were close in a more professional way because of football, but my mum and Sandra had a really strong, emotional bond. They were the glue of our family.

Nothing changes with Sandra and that's what I love and admire about her. She is so kind and has a good heart, and she has always been the same. She wants to protect people and my mum was very much like that too.

When we lost my mum, it was obviously very hard for us all and we were all suffering in our own ways, but for me, it was so nice to know that Sandra was there. When I speak to Sandra, she sounds so much like my mum and just hearing her voice reminds me of her and brings back such lovely memories.

I'm also very close to Harry, and I'd say when he was my boss at West Ham, it brought us closer together in some ways. My dad was quite firm on me, he was the assistant manager at the time, but I'd say Harry was somewhere in the middle ground. He was very supportive and I enjoyed playing for him. It was probably tougher for Harry than it was for me while we were working together. There was a lot of stuff about nepotism from the fans, and he was amazing at defending me and I really appreciated that. He wasn't afraid to say things that maybe others wouldn't and I think that's a trait a lot of people see in him now.

I admire Harry so much because of the job I do now, and the fact he did it for so long, and how he managed to keep up his energy and his wisdom towards it.

Even now, I lean on Harry and go to him for advice or in moments of work stress. When I was out of a job at Chelsea, I had a couple of opportunities come up and Harry was one of my first calls. I asked him what he thought and you know you will always get a well-informed and experienced answer from Harry. He was actually pivotal in me becoming a coach and he helped me out massively. I probably wouldn't have got my first job as a coach without him.

It's quite amazing how he has transcended from a football manager to a celebrity, and there aren't many people who can do that. I think in the jungle we all saw his true personality and he almost became a darling of the public. It's a special thing he has, but it's very natural to him.

Harry and Sandra have such an incredible marriage and I think it's probably down to balance. Harry has always been energetic, travelling here and there for work, and Sandra is an amazing home keeper, very much like my mum. They both love being in Bournemouth and it's where they are happiest. I know how much their family means to them, and they mean so much to us. I just hope they keep having a happy and healthy life together, and I'm so proud of them both.

Natalie Lampard, niece

I actually feel quite choked writing this. Sandra isn't just my aunt, but she is my best friend. She really is a wonderful person inside and out. We have got a beautiful relationship and we are very, very close. She is a very special woman to me and has helped me out in ways you couldn't ever know. She has been through the good times and the bad times with me, always by my side and always giving me good advice, lots of love and support. I will be forever grateful. Ten years ago, I was in a pretty bad place, but I came out of it to the other side because of my family. Sandra won't ever know the impact she has had on me, how she helped me overcome that bad period in my life, and how she has helped me be the person I am today. She truly is amazing.

Sandra is just so level-headed. Sandra and my mum Pat were so alike, except that Sandra was probably a bit more shy compared to my mum, who was always a bit more confident. But Sandra and my mum were like two peas in a pod.

I remember when I was at school, from the minute I woke up in the morning until when I came back home again, my mum and Sandra would be on the phone, chatting away. They were probably talking to each other all day and all evening too! They spoke about anything and everything and were so, so close. Back then you didn't have mobiles, so they would be chatting on the landline all day. I remember when the phone bill came in, my dad and Harry would always go mad as it was always really high. I remember them both being really excited when they introduced your 'favourite' numbers as it meant they could still talk to each other for ages but the phone bills would be cheaper!

Harry and my dad, Frank, were both football, football, football – we didn't have a chance to not like football in our houses. I'm nearly 52 and I still love it now.

As kids, I remember how we always used to go for our summer holidays down in Bournemouth. Sandra and Harry used to live in Old Barn Road in Christchurch, and we used to have a great time down there with my mum, my dad, my sister Claire and my brother Frank. They were the best summer holidays. We would also go down to Leysdown and spend time at Harry's parents' caravan. We used to have so much fun as kids. I hold all of those memories in my heart.

My mum and Sandra always used to joke how alike me and my cousin Mark were. We are only six months apart and his daughter Molly and my daughter Millie are six months apart, which is quite mad. And just like my mum and Sandra, we are like two peas in a pod. I remember whenever Mark got a spot as a kid, I'd get a spot too. Sandra would always say if something happened to Mark, there's a guarantee it would happen to me, too. It used to make them both laugh.

Me, my mum, Sandra and Claire would have girls' days out to Romford, where we would spend hours in the old-fashioned British Home Stores. We also used to go to this shop that was owned by a lovely lady called Gloria, who sold all types of designer clothes. They were not quite seconds, but had been worn by models, and she used to sell them at cheap prices. We would love it there and come away with bags full of clothes. And we have kept up that tradition as me, Sandra, Millie and Molly will meet up every couple of months and go shopping together in London.

I know it was a very heartbreaking and difficult time for Sandra when she lost my mum, it was for all of us. They were not just sisters, they really were the best of friends. I hope she knows that I am there for her like she has always been there for me. I also hope that I bring her a bit of comfort because she hasn't got my mum here any more.

One of the things I love the most about Sandra is that she will always hear two sides of every story. She always listens to me, and she will tell me when she thinks I am wrong. We just bounce off each other and are always having a laugh.

Sandra really does have a heart of gold and is very giving – she and Harry deserve all the happiness in the world, they really do. I don't know anyone who hasn't met them and not loved them.

I think they are very lucky to have each other – Harry in particular, haha! – and anyone would be lucky to have a marriage like they have.

I just want to wish my auntie and uncle lots of love. To Sandra and Harry, you continue to be an inspiration to both myself and Millie, and you both show us unconditional love always. You really are couple goals! And remember, love conquers all.

Emilie, granddaughter

Nanny and Pop mean so much to all of us. One of my favourite memories as a kid has to be pancakes in the morning after the sleepover at Nanny's house, playing in the garden and all of us with the FA Cup when Portsmouth won.

My nanny is the best. She can do anything and everything, no matter how she feels, and she's always so caring of others.

It's so hard to nail down what I admire about them the most, but one thing Pop said to us once was, "Be nice to everybody because there isn't anyone out there better than anyone else." I think that's a really important thing to remember and take with you every day. And I do.

Harry Jnr, grandson

To Nanny and Pop,

Thank you for always being there for me.

Pop for supporting me in football every week since I was six, to supporting me signing my first contract. Thank you for teaching me the ropes and inspiring me to work hard in my football.

Nanny, thank you for always being someone to talk to and making the best pancakes.

Love you both forever and always, Harry Jnr x.

Charley, grandson

Dear Nanny Wishie and Pop ,

I just wanted to say thank you so much for everything you have given everyone around you and thank you so much for always being there for all of us. And we are so proud of you both, thank you for everything,

Love you from Chazz Xx.

Beau, grandson

Dear Nan and Pop,

Thank you for everything over the years, especially Nanny for the amount of 'Tottenham cake' I would eat, as well as Pop for always helping me with my football and being an inspiration.

Love you guys xx

Lucy, daughter-in-law

If Carlsberg did in-laws it would be Harry and Sandra!

Thank you for all you have done for us:

Sandra, you have taught me so many things as a wife and mother, you have never judged but always been there for

244

advice and support through some of my biggest moments — even being a wonderful birthing partner to me.

Harry, thank you for your guidance and support. Being a wonderful grandad and making us all laugh so much, you are always there for everyone and fix everything. I will never forget what you did for me after my knee injury and I will continue to show my appreciation with home-made pie and mash for life!

Love you both very much.

Joe, grandson

Nanny and Pop have always been so kind to all of us. I love that they always played with me growing up, even if that entailed playing with me and my Nerf Guns! I love seeing them with my son, Hendrix. He absolutely adores them, they are so good with him. They are incredible grandparents and now great grandparents!

Thanks

To our sons Mark and Jamie, we are so proud of you both and what you have achieved. You have both gone from two football-mad young boys to two wonderful and loving husbands and fathers – albeit still football-mad! We have loved watching you start your own families and instil the values in your own children that we have with you, although maybe a little stricter!

We are so proud to call you our sons and we love you both so very much.

To our beautiful grandchildren Joe, Molly, Emilie, Charley, Harry, Beau, Bobbie and Raphael, and our great-grandson Hendrix, you are all amazing! You bring us so much joy and we are both very proud of each and every one of you. We feel so very lucky to watch you all grow up and it's an honour to be your Nanny and Pop. We love you all so much.

To our nieces Claire, Natalie and Sam and nephew Frank, you are like second children to us and we have so much love for you all. We have loved watching you become the wonderful adults you are today, and your mum, Pat, and dad, Brian, would be so, so proud of you. We are so lucky to have you and love you lots.

To our daughter-in-laws Lucy and Frida, thank you so much for everything you both do for Mark and Jamie and for giving us our beautiful grandchildren. And to Louise, thank you for being a wonderful daughter-in-law and helping to raise two fantastic boys. All three of you are very special to us.

To those we have lost, including our beloved Pat, life isn't the same without you. We miss your daily calls and think about you every day. We miss you so much and you will always be in our hearts.

To Brian, we miss our trips to Spain to see you and sharing a bottle of wine over a steak dinner. We will always hold those memories dear. We miss you.

To our nephew, Richard, you were taken far too soon but we were lucky to have you for over 40 years. You won't be forgotten.

To our own wonderful parents Harry and Violet and Betty and Bill, we hope we've done you proud. And you now see we made the right decision by buying a house! You will never know how special you were to us and we miss you all every single day. We love you.

To Lisa Jarvis, our ghostwriter, thank you so much for putting our story into words – we don't quite know how you did it! There have been lots of laughs and a few tears while writing this book together, but we have loved every minute of working with you. You have shown such kindness and have become a friend for life and for that we feel very lucky.

To our wonderful agent/publicist Scarlett Short, thank you for everything you do for us, and our granddaughter Molly. You are a fantastic role model to her and she has learned great things from you already. We really are so grateful for everything you do for us and we couldn't ask for a better publicist.

To Steve Hanrahan, Paul Dove, Rick Cooke, Claire Brown, Roy Gilfoyle, Richard Williamson and everyone at Mirror Books, thank you for your support over the past year and for letting us tell our story. We have enjoyed working so closely with you.

To our closest friends, we couldn't possibly name you all, but you know who you are! Thank you for your friendship, loyalty and support over the years. It means so much to us both and we are very lucky to be surrounded by such wonderful friends.

To the legendary Bobby Moore and George Best, your stars still shine so brightly. You were both taken far too soon and are sorely missed. We hope you are both having fun up there!

To Brian Tiler, we never got to thank you for everything you did for us. You were an amazing person and a true friend. You are forever in our hearts.

To Jim Smith, the best signing Harry ever made, you were a fantastic coach with so much wisdom and knowledge of the game, but most of all, we were very lucky to have you as a friend. We miss you dearly.

Mr & Mrs...

Who writes the Christmas cards?

Harry: Sandra.

Sandra: Me!

Who makes the first tea/coffee in the morning?

Harry: Sandra, but I get the croissants!

Sandra: Yes, I do, but Harry does at least know how to use the coffee machine!

Who is best at remembering birthdays?

Harry: Definitely Sandra, though I am good at remembering football scores, I just couldn't tell you the dates.

Sandra: Yes, me again.

Who looks after the passports at the airport?

Harry: Always Sandra.

Sandra: Definitely me, Harry would lose them!

What are you most likely to argue about?

Harry: I wouldn't say we argue, Sarn?

Sandra: Only about you making a mess in the kitchen!

Who answers the house phone?

Harry: I just about know how to work my mobile!

Sandra: It's usually me.

Who owns the remote control?

Harry: That will probably be me. But you watch your soaps, don't you Sarn?

Sandra: Sky Sports is on in the house all day.

Who waters the flowers?

Harry: I give it a go, I don't mind doing it.

Sandra: The last time you did you took the heads off my flowers with the jet wash!

Who puts up the Christmas tree and decorations?

Harry: I stay out of that one!

Sandra: I won't let him touch the tree.

Who will get the washing in if it's raining?

Harry: Oh yeah, Sandra.

Sandra: You would probably leave it out there!

Mr & Mrs...

Who empties the dishwasher the most?

Harry: Erm…

Sandra: I don't think you know we have one, Harry?

Do you have pet names for each other?

Harry: I've always called you Sarn, haven't I?

Sandra: Mr Pastry!

Who's best at saving money?

Harry: Sandra, but she is also good at spending it!

Sandra: I am a good saver!

Who takes the longest to get ready for a night out?

Harry: Not me, I take two minutes.

Sandra: Harry will leave it to the last minute to get ready, always.

Who picks new wallpaper or the colour of paint?

Harry: I wouldn't be trusted.

Sandra: No, no you wouldn't! I'd dread to think what our walls would look like!